HARD FACTS

HARD FACTS

Setting and Form
in the American Novel

Philip Fisher

New York   Oxford
OXFORD UNIVERSITY PRESS
1987

Oxford University Press, Walton Street, Oxford OX2 6DP

London New York Toronto
Delhi Bombay Calcutta Madras Karachi
Kuala Lumpur Singapore Hong Kong Tokyo
Nairobi Dar es Salaam Cape Town
Melbourne Auckland

and associated companies in
Beirut Berlin Ibadan Mexico City Nicosia

Copyright © 1985 by Oxford University Press, Inc.

First published in 1985 by Oxford University Press, Inc., 200 Madison Avenue
New York, New York 10016
First issued as an Oxford University Press paperback in 1987.

Library of Congress Cataloging in Publication Data

Fisher, Philip, 1941–
Hard facts.

Includes index.
1. American fiction—19th century—History and criticism. 2. Popular literature—United States—History
and criticism. 3. Setting (Literature) 4. Historical
fiction, American. 5. Sentimentalism in literature.
6. Slavery and slaves in literature. 7. Naturalism
in literature. 8. Cities and towns in literature.
I. Title.
PS377.F55 1985 813'.009 84-18999
ISBN 0-19-503528-3
0-19-504131-3 paperback

Permission has kindly been granted to reprint Robert Frost's poem "Spring
Pools" from *The Poetry of Robert Frost*, edited by Edward Connery Lathem.
Copyright 1928, © 1969 by Holt, Rinehart and Winston. Copyright © 1956 by
Robert Frost. Reprinted by permission of Holt, Rinehart and Winston,
Publishers.

Printing (last digit): 9 8 7 6 5 4 3 2

Printed in the United States of America

For
Elaine Scarry

Acknowledgments

Sections of the two final chapters of this book have appeared in earlier versions and I gratefully acknowledge permission to use them here: first, to the Johns Hopkins University Press for permission to reprint sections of Chapter 3 that appeared first in *ELH* and in *New Essays in American Realism*, edited by Eric Sundquist; second, to *Amerikastudien*, where an earlier version of part of Chapter 2 appeared. Finally, I am grateful to Holt, Rinehart and Winston for permission to reprint Robert Frost's poem "Spring Pools" from *The Poetry of Robert Frost*, edited by Edward Connery Lathem.

A number of perspectives and friendships have entered into the thinking from which this book emerged, and I would like to acknowledge them here.

I am especially grateful to Daniel Aaron whose wide knowledge, sharp response, encouragement, and enthusiasm, as well as his great pleasure in the exchange of ideas, often while bicycling along the streets of Boston and Cambridge, have played an important role in the making of this book.

For more than ten years I have been unusually privileged to enjoy the energy of the intellectual life of my colleagues at Brandeis and their warm friendship as well. To Michael Gilmore, Allen Grossman, Robert Preyer, and Eugene Goodheart, my special thanks.

The perspective of this book owes a great deal to the fresh view of American culture provided by a semester of teaching at the John F. Kennedy Institut of the Frei Universitat, Berlin. To Heinz Ickstadt and Winfried Fluck who extended the invitation that made that new distance possible and elicited the lecture on *Uncle Tom's Cabin* that shaped the middle section of this book, my gratitude. For conversations and the lively exchange of ideas in Berlin, I am grateful to them as well as to Ursula Brumm and Michael Hoenisch. I also want to thank Olaf Hansen of the Goethe Universitat, Frankfurt, whose friendship has shaped my sense of the outside perspective on America over the past eight years.

Another outside perspective was a generational one, and I am grateful to my son Mark for his lively arguments and high spirits.

Finally, all of these perspectives are surrounded and made intellectually rich by the woman to whom this book is dedicated, Elaine Scarry, who has been and is pleasure and frame, anchor and sail.

1984   P. F.

Contents

HARD FACTS

Introduction

When we speak of the work done by culture, it is usually of what culture does with and for the past that we are thinking. Culture, as we commonly say, articulates, in the sense of giving shape to and sorting out, some part of the past as it can be of use to a particular present. It locates the few best instances and makes of them the "classics." A classic is, by definition, the one thing that no work can be in its own time. In the same way, the one thing that no poet writing in what we have come to call the Romantic period could choose to be, or experience himself as being, was a "Romantic Poet." Both the selecting out of classic instances and the shaping of effective retroactive categories are the cultural work, done for itself, that every present executes on the past.

There is another meaning to the work of culture when we consider what the present does in the face of itself, for itself, and not for any possible future. Culture, in this sense, does work that, once done, becomes obvious and unrecoverable because it has become part of the habit structure of everyday perception. Within the present, culture stabilizes and incorporates nearly ungraspable or widely various states of moral or representational or perceptual experience. It changes again and again what the census of the human world looks like— what it includes or excludes—and it often does so in tandem with changes in social fact or legal categories that make, from the standpoint of a later perspective, the facts seem obvious. The end of slavery as a legal and military fact in America was, in this sense, a partner term to the insistence by Stowe, in *Uncle Tom's Cabin*, on human representability for black Americans.

After the legal act of the Emancipation Proclamation, after the military victory of the Union and the cultural work of *Uncle Tom's Cabin*, blacks were no longer "things," and therefore property, but persons. The redesign of the boundary between the categories of man and thing was an act of cultural work, as well as a legal and military matter, because the moral and perceptual change that alone could make effective a formal change had to be done by means of moral and perceptual practice, which includes repetition and even memorization. Where culture installs new habits of moral perception, such as the recognition that a child is a person, a black is a person, it accomplishes, as a last step, the forgetting of its own strenuous work so that what are newly learned habits are only remembered as facts. Once what had only recently been a risky and disputable claim has come to seem obvious, the highest work of culture has been done, but because the last step involves forgetting both the process and its very openness to alternatives or to failure, the history of culture has trouble in later remembering what it is socially and psychologically decisive for it to forget.

While the examples of slavery and childhood in the 19th century might be taken to imply that the redesign of categories within culture takes place primarily in a liberal direction, the fact is that the work of culture includes equally powerful value-free changes and, at the other extreme, the installation of such categories as "the Barbarian," "the Pagan," or "the Jew" within cultures where the categories exist only to isolate out targets. In the same way, the transformation of terms or the separation out of figures for moral or political attention has as its alternative cultural moments of what should be called a "collapse of categories." Within 19th-century America the policy of removing the Indians and, later, confining them to reservations, had in the background the collapse of differences, in the white mind, so that Apaches and Creeks, farming and hunting nations, Christianized and savage, no matter what their differences or dangers, were simply designated "Indians" and subjected to a common fate. The very choice within a culture to attend to increasingly refined differences or to more and more inclusive categories is a political act for which the inner practice and memorization takes place informally and continuously.

The simple argument of this book is that within the 19th-century American novel, cultural work of this fundamental kind was often done by exactly those popular forms that from a later perspective, that of 20th-century modernism, have seemed the weakest features of 19th-century cultural life. What I have chosen to look at here are three of the central hard facts of American history: the killing of the Indians, which gave a "clear land" where a "new world" might be built; the slavery that was a moral and rational outrage in a society picturing itself in Jeffersonian terms as a nation of free and independent yeoman farmers; and, finally, the severe evacuation and objectification of the self that followed from the economic and future-oriented world of capitalism and the city.

For each of these three hard facts of American reality the work of culture included a number of features. First, for those who were within the culture and had as yet no account, it created an almost dream-like simplification in which, nonetheless, the most troubled and volatile features of the whole were preserved intact. The very impact of the new representation derived from this simplification and condensation. *Uncle Tom's Cabin* is the most profound example of this act of condensation. No other book has so openly laid siege to the crowded space of representation and set its facts within by occupying an uneraseable part of that space. The international popularity of Stowe's book, the plays and recitations, illustrations and cultural clichés derived from it, installed the slave system in the public realm.

My interest here is in three writers whose goal was this act of inserting into the already filled moral and cultural realm one new reality. The strategies of this act seem to me to be the most radical of which culture is capable. Cooper "made up" the wilderness; the Indian and the killing of the Indian; the process of settlement and, along with that process, the single white figure, Leatherstocking, who made morally tolerable the ethical complexities of settlement and the superseding of the Indians that was the basic secondary fact within settlement. To say that Cooper "made up" this reality is only to say that he was able to lodge the details, the settings and the characters, the moral pride and moral shame of this history in the imagination of the American and European world, and that later representations drew on the history that he made symbolically concrete.

In the same way, Dreiser inserts the urban world as an array of psychological habits, perceptual events, forms of action and details of timing and structure into a literary form that had, before him, only understood the moral and representational peculiarities of urban life as a set of defective variations of what it took to be the only "real life": that lived by small, closed communities acting under the pressures of moral codes, behavioral patterns, and principles of knowledge and judgment. The city of capitalism, of economics and of self-making, of what I will call the "life history of objects," is an entirely new fact and one as morally convoluted as the history of settlement that Cooper devised and the history of that Jeffersonian ideal of yeoman farmers into which Stowe built the reality of slavery.

That Dreiser introduces into the imagination, at the same time, a new central type, one as culturally central as Don Quixote or Faust, and that his instance is a woman who rises in a dynamic world, an actress, suggests that new territories of imaginative space are always locked into place, in part, by means of a single central person. Often this figure is of a puzzling blankness or passivity: as Leatherstocking, Uncle Tom, and Dreiser's Carrie all are. Later periods often find such figures wooden, offensive, and trite. Like Uncle Tom, once they have carried out their radical capture of imaginative space, they become themselves political targets of every later mind privileged to look out through the structure that would never have existed without those very elements that now seem so offensive. A figure like Uncle Tom is a window that becomes, in time, itself visible so that, in staring *at* it, it is easy to forget that, initially, it was easy to look through this opening into a world that had been both concealed and unstructured.

In this sense, I am writing here about three cultural acts that by their very success made themselves obsolete, and perhaps even a hindrance, once their cultural work was complete. One of my goals is to recover and name the work that they did, and to understand the capacity of popular forms to accomplish just this self-terminating work of the imagination. The historical novel, the sentimental novel, and the naturalist novel are three of the forms with which the weakness of 19th-century culture is, when seen from the perspective of 20th-century modernism, most often identified. It is my claim that these forms were not forms for the future, but forms for the active transformation of the present. Such work within the present can be summarized in the terms that Freud used for therapy: recognition, repetition, and working through. The matter of communal life can not, any more than can that of individual life, be forgotten, repressed, or tolerated only in its variety of disguises. The scenes of common life undergo moments of recognition just as Oedipus, at last, comes to own up to and therefore to own what his life has been and is.

Popular forms are frequently repetitive, and they are frequently read almost obsessively, as detective novels, westerns, romances, and pornography are, becoming part of what might be called a diet of reality that returns again and again to the same few motifs so that they might not slip away. Cooper's great invention led to the yearly crop of Westerns and shoot-em-ups that repeat on and on the fact of killing, which is one of the central, inaugural facts of American life. Repetition is in the service of working through or at least in the service of refusing to forget. All three acts, recognition, repetition, and working through, are features of cultural incorporation. Only a few facts keep on being remembered as who we are and those facts are incorporated and then, after a time, felt to be obvious and even trite.

The cultural work required to make Uncle Tom trite is paradoxically the most sophisticated process of social life. In this sense, my concern, in looking at these three cultural acts, is to try to rediscover the moment of setting in place part of the framework of national self-imagination, and to argue that the act of compromise or sympathy with ordinary perception and common states of feeling that made it possible for Cooper or Stowe or Dreiser to build that aspect of self-consciousness is the central act of cultural work, when it is done, not for the future, but for the transformation of whatever present appears unstructured, or, alternatively, fixed and representationally crowded. Literally, what is unstructured or excluded is un-imaginable. The cultural work that I am describing is the process by which the unimaginable becomes, finally, the obvious. It is the ordinariness of Cooper and Stowe and Dreiser that permits them a transforming power unavailable to the "genius" of Melville, Dickinson, or James who, for all of their extraordinary and dense *uniqueness*, were unable to bring about the work of the cultural present. I am using the word "ordinary" in a sense that has now lost its authority. I intend it to convey the universality of the everyday. Ordinariness suggests that which is central and accurate. It is in this sense of "ordinary" that, for example, 20th-century analytic phi-losophy has taught us that ordinary language carries and imposes the deepest imperatives of our long-standing philo-sophical choices. Ordinary language, and the ordinary habits of perception and acknowledgement that such language records and perpetuates, are redesigned at every cultural moment. The ambition to redesign the common world is the ambition of the best instances of cultural work.

1. PRIVILEGED SETTINGS

Every history has, in addition to its actual sites, a small list of privileged settings. These are not at all the places where key events have taken place. Instead, they are ideal and simplified vanishing points toward which lines of sight and projects of every kind converge. From these vanishing points, the many approximate or bungled, actual states of affairs draw order and position. Whatever actually appears within a society can be interpreted as some variant, some anticipation or displacement or ruin, of one of these privileged settings.

The images or myths described by such earlier writers as Henry Nash Smith in *Virgin Land* or Leo Marx in *The Machine in the Garden* play the role of what I am calling privileged settings. Leo Marx has summarized the work done by what he refers to as "symbolic landscapes" when he describes how the wilderness

> activated the stubborn settlers who struggled for years to raise crops in what was literally a desert; it led congressmen to insist upon certain impractical provisions of the Homestead Act; it lay back of the peculiarly bitter frustration of western farmers beginning in the 1870s; it kept alive the memory of Thomas Jefferson; it caused artists and writers both popular and serious to lose touch, as time went on, with social realities; it excited the imagination of Frederick Jackson Turner, not to mention all the historians who so eagerly endorsed the "frontier hypothesis" as the most plausible explanation for the Americanness of various attitudes and institutions—and one could go on.[1]

For America, these settings have had an unusual force, because of the need for vanishing points and guiding patterns during the rapid construction of the culture, and at the same time, an unusually treacherous relation to hard facts. American culture has had nonetheless a vigorous appetite for a tough-minded restaging of the central facts of its history. Three principal settings have provided vanishing points for American history. Each has embedded within it a central fact and each has, within literature, elicited an imaginative account within one of the deliberately "popular" forms that provided a fixed pattern of figures and acts around which imagination and debate, policy and dreaming could occur. The settings are: first, the wilderness with its hard fact of the Indian and its popular form, the historical novel; second, the modest homestead or family farm with its corrosive fact of slavery and its appropriate form, the sentimental novel; third, the city with its core reality of the object world and exchange patterns and its popular form in the naturalist novel invented by Zola and given American form by Dreiser.

To be more precise, these settings should be described as: the already partially conquered wilderness; the independent, stable family-sized homestead or farm; and the half-built city. The wilderness is always understood as vanishing or threatened. The grandeur that is the central theme of every description of those who first step into it always has been accompanied by an element of regret, since their very presence signals the oncoming wave that will destroy it. Whatever its power is, it is seen as short-lived and fragile because it is less than the power of any man with a sharp ax. The vanishing wilderness, as a setting, encodes a certain guilt about the process of settlement and conquest, by placing in the foreground the fact that construction only occurs through the destruction of greatness. Civilization is always a replacement, a supersession. Among many other things, this permits the wilderness as a setting to stand in for a morally troubling set of human facts. In particular, it encodes the fact that white culture in America replaces a prior, noble culture. It is built by means of the simultaneous destruction of Indian culture.

For Cooper it is the forest that condenses these emotional facts of wonder and regret. Tall, long-rooted trees are the prominent feature of his wilderness descriptions. As isolated, free-standing objects, trees have an individuality that lets them easily represent, or have the feel of, persons. Indians and trees are both described in similar terms: tall, erect, noble, ancient. The cutting down of a tree and the "cutting down" of an Indian are surrogate acts for one another. Similarly, in *The Oregon Trail*, Parkman so closely models his descriptions of the herds of buffalo and the bands of Indians on one another, that the great slaughter of buffalo that ends his book has a latent resonance as a description of an Indian massacre. From the great trees of Cooper's forest descriptions come the cabins of the settlers. The facts of destruction and supersession, both of the material world and of the human world, are summed up by the pair of images: a forest, then a log cabin in a clearing.

The wilderness is the privileged setting of beginnings, both national and individual. In its later forms, as in the West or Walden Pond or the setting of Hemingway's "Big Two-Hearted River," it is the setting in which to begin again. Beginnings, fresh starts, even brief renewals gain design from what is projected in an ideal form as wilderness. The hard fact of the wilderness is one which Darwin made the 19th century able to remember: it was not empty. To clear it meant to kill off or move out the Indians who were already there. This in turn meant that the genuine first act was a murderous one that might be pictured as having taken place just before the first stakes were driven into the ground. The beginning within the wilderness came provided with a pre-history that had the structure of an ending.

This pattern is so imbedded in the American imagination that it can be tacitly assumed. In Hemingway's classic story "Big Two-Hearted River," the narrative of the wilderness does not mention the recent war that precedes the action of the narrative. The off-stage killing has ended, but the fresh, pure beginning is shaped by its unstated reality.

Where the wilderness is a setting of origins, the farm, particularly in the Jeffersonian ideal of a nation of independent, small, self-sufficient, family farms, is a setting that represents an ideal stability. A nation of free, democratic individuals who are satisfied and therefore not driven to increase their holdings or to seek ever greater profits makes possible an unchanging balance between man and nature and between man and his fellow citizens. The Jeffersonian setting, written into law in the Homestead Act after the Civil War, provided a privileged setting for the present and a form of the present that might always be the present, just as the wilderness had set in place the past and its pre-history. The ephemeral and regrettable fragility of the wilderness is reversed by the perpetuity of farm and family. The hard fact within the Jeffersonian setting was slavery. This setting celebrated independence and underlined the close connection of hard work, self-sufficiency, and rural life to political democracy and freedom. Jefferson made political forms dependent upon economic forms, insofar as they patterned daily life. Yet within America, this privileged setting with its crucial implications for the viability of the political side of democratic life, contained within it the most pervasive system of slavery found in any Europeanized nation.

The third setting could be called the city of opportunity. The city is the privileged setting of possibility, of "about-to-be" realized future states. The city is the future in a physical form. Since America itself, throughout the 19th century, was still incomplete, the partially built city could serve as a profound national image in a way that would not be true for other countries. In numbers of states, in institutional and cultural structures, in basic patterns of laws and behavior, even in numbers, the United States was a prospect rather than a reality until early in the 20th century. The city is unstable, not only in the sense of being only partially built, but more importantly because it includes the dynamic assumption of individual fortunes that hold out the possibility of rising to the top or failing to rise, falling or losing one's footing. Not the family, but the individual is the central actor within the privileged setting of the city. Neither moral choices nor patterns of manners, but careers give the scheme of action.

The city is the setting for a version of life that has its structure in an economy, as the Jeffersonian farm is the setting for a life based within a political society, and the wilderness, a life set within nature. The structuring base of economy, political society, or nature is built into the conditions of the half-built city, the family farm, and the vanishing wilderness. Just as the wilderness included the primary fact that it was not empty but already ordered and pre-empted, and just as political society, while ideologically universal, had always been, in fact, the beneficiary of a large base of nonmembers such as slaves, women, and children, so the economy, as the base from which the urban setting drew its form, had at its center the fact of exchange. At the risk of simplification, exchange demands that everything that is gotten must come from somewhere else. Every rise has in its background a complementary fall. Every seller who has profited by selling high must be matched by a buyer whose misfortune it was to have had to pay through the nose.

The psychological implications of what, for the setting of the city, might be called the "half-made" man, rather than the "self-made" man, or the futurization of the self, are features of the economic setting. Finally, the domination of the structure of things and the necessity within an economic setting to consider oneself, at least in part, as a thing that must be sold or can be advertised or packaged, makes up a further aspect of the city as a privileged setting. As Dreiser discovered, this new self-relation is best embodied in the life of an actress, who both is and is not her many roles, who rises or falls and can become a star or a nobody, and who must merchandise herself as any new product is merchandised.

Each of these three popular forms dictates the central human agent by which the reality can be deciphered. For the city it is that most intensified free agent: the late-adolescent girl or young woman whose many temporary possibilities are best named roles. Character or personality are too fixed and cumulative to describe this new, mobile individualism. For the Jeffersonian farm of Stowe's novel the central agent is the black family and only secondarily its separated members. The homestead or location in which family life can occur is named ironically in Stowe's title: *Uncle Tom's Cabin*. This is a cabin that they ought to own and live in, as the possessive "Tom's" indicates. But, since they are themselves possessions and there-fore victims of the acts and choices of others, the family cabin is the one place that Uncle Tom can never get to throughout the course of the novel, and it is a thing that, because in Stowe's subtitle he is "a man that was a thing," he cannot own. Where the individual, in the modern economic sense of that term, is the decisive agent of the urban novel, and the black family with its emptied home, the decisive agent of the sentimental novel, in Cooper's case, and for the historical novel in general, it is the pair of men linked by the bond of killing, that defines the central agent. Since the history of this male bond with its blend of friendship and killing has been traced by Leslie Fiedler and others, and now makes up one of the accepted patterns of American cultural analysis, it can be stated here without calling up its details. For the wilderness as a privileged setting this male pair is as structurally definitive as the family is in the setting of rural, sentimental life, and as the free individual, young and versatile—or, as we say in ordinary language, "promising"—is for the capitalist city.

2. Popular Forms

No writer is as close to a master key to the entire 19th-century European and American novel as Sir Walter Scott with his invention of the historical novel. This form developed and gained mythic and philosophical power in the works of Cooper, Hugo, Tolstoy, and Eliot. Allied to the political force of nationalism and to the later regionalisms, it became a vehicle for claiming and defining a national identity. Reality of time and place, of moment and milieu, are its overriding central matters. Applied as a technique to the present rather than to the past, the historical novel made possible Balzac and Flaubert, Hardy, Dreiser, and Mann. The historical novel gives a new priority to description over event and moral character. It elevates the setting, both of time and of place, to a prominent position. But more importantly, it redefines setting as an environment intended to be rationally understood as a set of forms, of local customs, of habits of mind and behavior, of moral styles and, most importantly of all, of rival forces engaged in open or hidden warfare. The environment of a typical historical novel is a complete and non-universal "world." The world of a small area of American forest in Cooper or the world of the coal mine in Zola's *Germinal* or the world of the sanitorium in Mann's *The Magic Mountain* are three classic examples. Each world has its rules and inner logic, its ethos and typical events.

As Lukács has shown, the historical novel transforms our notion of character by replacing moral individuality, or personality, with a more historical and deterministic notion of type and typicality.[2] It brings a certain abstractness and blankness into character in order to make the choices and temperaments comprehensible as products of a given society and moment. Along with the descriptive power of the type in the realm of character, the historical novel imposed an event structure of action that miniaturized or localized the larger significant play of forces and their long-term outcome. Such miniaturization gave the plot of historical novels an almost allegorical feel. The local moment and events so completely embodied the larger national or social struggle that the plot could be read as a coded version of the larger social world.[3]

Finally, the historical form was committed to a dynamic reality whose central feature was warfare. Examples of this warfare are the warfare of white and Indian in Cooper's novels, of Scot and Englishman in the Waverly novels, of Russia and France in Tolstoy. More internally, the struggle between classes, between codes no longer tolerant of one another or even between ways of life, as in the struggle between burgher and artist in Mann's *Buddenbrooks*, are more subtle forms of warfare. The historical novel's emphasis on decisive and deadly struggle, linked to an already known clear outcome, made it the vehicle for the ready incorporation of Darwinism and other biological descriptions that replaced the image of nature as an ordered world with a dynamic and murderous, historicized account of an ever-changing short-term balance.

The naturalist novel of Zola and Dreiser represents a specialized variant of Scott's form. It is, we might say, Scott's form tailored for a public world that is an economy rather than a polis. For Scott, Cooper, or Tolstoy, the public realm is still a kingdom in many ways continuous with the world of Shakespeare's history plays. Structured by families, concerned with power rather than money, centralized or capable of centralization, with action that radiates outward, such worlds are strongly pre-economic, even non-economic. Zola saw that the world given to him for description was a world most easily divided into worlds of work and profession. The "world" of a department store, of a coal mine, the world of art or of the Paris food markets, the world of the military or the theater: each sector of the economic map has its local features, types, common language, heroes, and catastrophes. The development visible in Zola and Dreiser, and which we now call the naturalist novel, was an inevitable development once the primary plane of social life became economic rather than political, atomized rather than centered, focused on money rather than on power, and based in the lives of individuals rather than families.

The strongly scientific, biological underpinnings of this form cast the novel as a form of research. No longer was the aristocratic, amateur, antiquarian pose of Scott enough. The feeling of necessity or the amoral, deterministic elements of Zola and Dreiser are translations, as I will show in the final chapter, not so much of a pessimism about the individual will, as of a profoundly scaled accommodation to lived, physical life as opposed to moral or social life.

The naturalist form that took its starting point in an environment quickly became the essential popular form. Modern best-sellers set in airports and hospitals, communes or political campaigns, with their appropriate character types and events, vocabularies and ethos, remain so common precisely because Zola's form contained the matching features for a society that had turned into an economy which could be subdivided into worlds, with free and mobile individuals as the main social actors.

One part of the transition from the earlier historical form of Scott and Cooper to the economic form of Zola and Dreiser can clearly be seen in Stowe's *Uncle Tom's Cabin*. Because her subject was slavery and her goal was social transformation, Stowe was committed to the sentimental form of the novel. The details of the politically radical technique of sentimentality will be elaborated in the analysis of the novel itself. However, because slavery is a form of work as well as a way of life, an economic relation as well as a relation of power, a thing-relation as well as a personal relation, Stowe's novel had a second dimension. Its texture is sentimental but its structure is naturalist. Hers is a novel of research, of typical facts and cases. She spends great effort creating the character types and varieties of moral life that must inevitably follow from the system of slavery. In doing this she gives the anatomy of her subject, slavery, and that anatomy becomes the structure of her novel. Its three parts are based in the three primary economic kinds of slavery: first, the few slaves associated with a family farm; second, the household slavery of domestic urban life; third, the plantation system of the deep south. Her novel, to accomplish its cultural work, reaches out to combine the two most resonant popular forms of the century, the sentimental form and the historical form, half-way in its transition to an economic rather than a political model. The inner logic of the historical novel grew out of the requirements of late moments of consciousness. The history of earlier events was written from a moment when a strong sense of destiny and inevitability had taken over about the final outcome. Once Manifest Destiny, or the Course of Empire, or the decline or vanishing of a civilization, had advanced so far that its conclusion was unmistakable, the representation of the past could not avoid scenes that became emblems or previews of what the later time knew to be oncoming. Scott writes from the point of view of the end point of Scottish identity. Cooper celebrates the newly vanished wilderness, pioneer, and Indian of the East.

In this sense the historical novel is a device for practicing how to meet a certain but postponed future. It is a psychological rehearsal that creates an ordered resignation that lets a group "face," as we put it, a future that they have already chosen and set in motion, but have not yet morally or psychologically passed through. The historical novel trains resignation and gives an elevated moral tone to stoic regret. It pictures forces as beyond control, already underway, and creates central figures who embody processes they do not control.

The historical novel is the complementary form to the more radical sentimental novel which trains and explicates new forms of feeling. As popular forms within 19th-century culture, the pair of forms maps out the two political possibilities for action. The sentimental novel arouses and excites action toward that part of the public future that is still open to decision and alternatives—slavery in the America of *Uncle Tom's Cabin*, the child in the England of Dickens and Words-worth. The historical novel makes profound and acceptable acts of resignation in the face of that part of the future that has already been determined but not yet achieved, and in the face of which action is futile. The sentimental novel, as a radical form of popular transformation, has its inevitable American subject in slavery and black experience. In the same way, the conservative, tragic form of the historical novel, equally a form that prepares consciousness and *designs* the frame of images with which a society faces its experience, found in America its inevitable moment 1820–40 and its subject, the Indian.

The distinction that formerly was made between high and popular culture, between art and kitsch (a category in which most people would still put the Leatherstocking Tales of Cooper and *Uncle Tom's Cabin*), involved the claim that art invented patterns of feeling while kitsch with its stereotypes and familiar feelings played to the appetites already in existence. Popular forms like the sentimental novel and the historical novel soothed by means of the familiar, it was claimed, and ultimately they dulled the sensibilities that art made lively by means of its "advanced" and innovative configurations. But when we look back candidly we can see that often the popular forms, while stale in detail and texture, were massing small patterns of feeling in entirely new directions. The wilderness, the Indian, the Frontiersman, the action of hunting, killing, and rescuing, became articulated in Cooper's novels by means of a texture of small moral, emotional, and narrative clichés. Slavery, and with it the moral geography of black-white relations, the hollowing out from within of the Jeffersonian ideal of a nation of independent yeoman farmers which was at the same time a nation of slave relations—these are displayed and locked into focus in Stowe's sentimental novel by means of a texture of commonplace feelings and acts. This "making familiar" should be seen as the counter-term to the so much discussed "defamiliarization" or "estrangement" that the Russian formalist Shklovsky proposed as the central act of culture.[4] Making familiar or making ordinary is the radical "work" done by popular forms.

The high art forms, like the novels of manners of James or the allegories of Hawthorne, are territorially late. They build nuances of texture, structure, detail, and psychology into nearly exhausted terrains. The popular forms colonize entirely new terrains. They enter what are only temporarily exotic configurations of experience as a necessary practice for a transformation of moral life that is approaching. This can occur either as a prelude and practice for moral action, as *Uncle Tom's Cabin* creates the inner resolve and the moral bond that makes fighting the Civil War comprehensible; or as a practice of mourning and resignation, as Cooper's novels and Parkman's histories do for the destruction of the wilderness and the removal of the Indians.

In popular forms images outrun analysis. The opposite is true in high art. The intricate and surprising, complex analysis lavished on a set of frail visual moments in Hawthorne or James elevates the work itself to a critical disquisition upon its own materials. The works of George Eliot, James, Conrad, and Faulkner epitomize the modernist ideal of the novel because within the novels themselves can be found the secondary analyses of their own exhausted categories—heroism, manners, selfishness, marriage. They are themselves disquisitions, critical speculation of a profound kind, about their own material. The popular forms, sentimental, historical, and naturalist, often seem, when quoted in moments of self-analysis, stupid, obtuse, commonplace. Dreiser's wisdom, as he reflects on what he has imagined, Zola's, Cooper's, or Scott's analysis of the patterns each has pictured, is never sharp and interesting *per se*. Instead it is the picture-making, the configurations and patterns themselves, that are entirely fresh and particularly in need of later, external analysis because, by being so striking, they quickly became settled in the language and in the perceptual frame of their civilization. To a later eye they appear obvious, even stale. Such images invaded and then ordered massive, unsorted psychic materials. Cooper's Indians and frontiersmen, Stowe's Topsy and Uncle

Tom, Dreiser's Carrie, colonized so quickly the national mind that they came rapidly to seem an entrenched burden that served as a barrier to the intelligent perceptions that they themselves had initially made possible. As focusing devices, Uncle Tom or Leatherstocking, Topsy or Chingachgook seem barriers and simplifying clichés to the very people taught to look in certain directions by means of these lenses and to discover order and psychic familiarity in territories earlier approached only as confusing no-man's-lands. The economic layer of life without which any account of the city is merely moral and trivial required the popular form of Dreiser and remained utterly untouched by the high cultural attempts of James's *The Bostonians* and Howells's *A Hazard of New Fortunes*.

High culture of the kind represented by Hawthorne, Melville, James, and Howells remains unincorporated and therefore it remains as fresh and extra-ordinary as when it was written. The works and writers that I wish to examine here are examples of culture that invites and then achieves incorporation. Because so much of its reality has leaked out and merged into the common language of perception and moral action, its very success, as mimesis, in altering the categories of reality, hides the extra-ordinary energy that now seems already ours.

1

Killing a Man:
The Historical Novel and the
Closing Down of Pre-History

To describe the 1840s in America we might revise Gertrude Stein's phrase about Oakland and say that by 1850, for the United States, there was at last a "there" there. With the Mexican War, the Southwest from Texas to California was complete. As a result of the gold rush and the Oregon migration, the West Coast from north to south had begun to be occupied. The continental interior was now surrounded and America was "there."

At the cultural level, the French had long ago been defeated and their great holdings bought out in the Louisiana Purchase. The Spanish had now lost California and the Southwest. Anglo-American culture alone had survived. The two great internal political differences, slavery and the sovereign Indian nations, were on their way to defeat. What was "there" as geography, culture, and political sovereignty was a state of hard fact, very different from what might earlier have been described as the promise or the idea of America. The earlier promise had been a philosophical matter and had therefore generated theoretical debate. This state of fact, for its part, invited history, historical myths of origins and cultural analysis. It naturally produced *The Song of Hiawatha* rather than *The Federalist Papers*, Parkman rather than Jefferson, the novels of Cooper instead of the Declaration of Independence.

Between 1835 and 1850 a sharply drawn historical map of this state of fact was produced. In the years between Tocqueville's *Democracy in America* of 1835 and Parkman's *The Conspiracy of Pontiac* of 1851 were published the first three volumes of Bancroft's *History of the United States*, the final two novels of Cooper's "Leatherstocking Tales," and Parkman's ingenious *The Oregon Trail*. Bancroft's volumes defined the standard colonial history, the pre-history of the political entity called the United States. Cooper's novels reconstructed the mythic first stages of settlement, and in Parkman's travel romance, the journey west was made to model going back in time historically to the central facts and relations that were also those of Cooper's novels: the wilderness; the stages of arrival, exploration, and settlement; the Indian; the acts of hunting and killing. Just as Thoreau was able at Walden Pond between July 4, 1845, and September 6, 1847, by a geographical dislocation of a little over a mile, to reconstitute the earliest conditions of settlement and wilderness, water and land, building and farming, so too Parkman, in the same year, 1846, went west into the past. Such a recovery of beginnings was also the essence of Bancroft's three colonial volumes, and of Cooper's final two novels of the Leatherstocking Sequence, novels that dealt with the earliest stages of Bumppo's life and simultaneously with the symbolic reenactment of the earliest phases of national history for which that life is a surrogate. An equivalent recovery of origins occupied Parkman's historical tragedy, *The Conspiracy of Pontiac*, in which the final defeat of the French in the 1750s and the preview of the failure of Indian resistance to American encroachment miniaturized the series of losses and withdrawals that would clear the land for the American presence.

In both Parkman and Cooper it is defeat and vanishing that the surface of the narrative chronicles. The celebration of the winners is implicit but banished from the surface where a defeated, primitive nobility occupies the center. That the wilderness, the buffalo, the Indians, even in the act of conquest and slaughter, define the centers of narratives that elude moral categories as though by design suggests just how sophisticated a frame has been set in place for a core of hard facts that are, at an ethical or humanistic level, brutal and murderous. One of the most popular long poems ever written in America, Longfellow's *The Song of Hiawatha* of 1855, a poem that unfortunately is as close to a national epic poem as we are ever likely to have, relies on a similar surface fascination with Indian life at the moment just before the appearance of the white civilization that would supercede it. The death or departure of Hiawatha ends the poem and coincides with the arrival of the first white missionaries with their "new world." A massacre of Indians ends Cooper's *The Deerslayer.* An almost senselessly extended massacre of buffalo, clearly felt as partners to and surrogates for the Indians, concludes *The Oregon Trail.* The death of Pontiac and the slaughter of the tribe of his murderers ends Parkman's history. In each case narratives that recover and mythologize national beginnings have, instead of inaugural acts, profoundly felt murderous endings. These endings are, from the point of view of their contemporary reader, beginnings both of the nation that a reader of 1845 is part of, and of a bloody Indian conquest that by the reader's time was reaching a climax.

The phrase "Manifest Destiny" was first used in July of 1845, and it is for the origin of what by then seemed destined that Cooper, Parkman, Bancroft, Longfellow, and Tocqueville reached back.[1] The well-known prophetic, final paragraph of Tocqueville's first volume is typical in its tone of fate and destiny.

> There are at the present time two great nations in the world, which started from different points, but seem to tend towards the same end. I allude to the Russians and the Americans . . . these alone are proceeding with ease and celerity along a path to which no limit can be perceived. The American struggles against the obstacles that nature opposes to him; the adversaries of the Russian are men. The former combats the wilderness and savage life; the latter, civilization with all its arms . . . the

principal interest of the former is freedom; of the latter, servitude. Their starting point is different and their courses are not the same; yet each of them seems marked out by the will of Heaven to sway the destinies of half the globe.[2]

Dealing as he is in 1835 with nascent realities and the visionary conclusions of destinies just underway, Tocqueville employs the somber, even ominous tone of a middle moment from which he can see with equal clarity backward to the decisive features of the beginning and forward to the already-outlined state of completion. Writing as he is for Europeans, the central matter of his conclusion is the eclipse of the western European nations. Parkman's *The Conspiracy of Pontiac* ends with the identical prophetic sweep.

> Neither mound or tablet marked the burial place of Pontiac. For a mausoleum a city has risen above the forest hero; and the race whom he hated with such burning rancor tramples with unceasing footsteps over his forgotten grave.[3]

Here Parkman doubles the intensity of political failure and personal death. He deepens even the racial, general death of extinction by evoking a future obliteration in which the memories and traces of groups are as lost as they themselves. The multiple death of a "forgotten grave" foresees that they will be abolished from the mind as they have already been cleared from the earth.

The power of the slogan "Manifest Destiny" lies in its first word, since it is only at a certain moment that the future becomes evident and inevitable and that then, as a result, the past can be sorted into, on the one hand, significant features that contributed to the founding of what can now be seen to be the future and, on the other hand, historical debris, fruitless possibilities that will never be realized. Once destiny is manifest, and is felt by consensus to be manifest, the writing of history can begin. Bancroft, Parkman, Tocqueville, and Cooper are made possible. The fictionalizing of origins, the convergence of events into stories, the thickening of pictorial images into emblems that richly condense what is known to be the original states of being are all made possible by the same moment of manifest destiny. The story of King Oedipus is, after all, the story of a destiny that is manifest too early (as prophecy that is rejected) and too late (as conviction for crimes already, but unconsciously done) but never manifested at the moment of action itself. In American experience the moment between 1835 and 1850 is one in which names and slogans, historical and mythic reconstruction, as well as personal, experiential reenactments, such as those of Parkman and Thoreau, arrive simultaneously with the freezing into place of a situation of hard and irrevocable fact.

1. BEGINNINGS THAT HIDE ENDINGS

The historical consciousness of the 1840s returned to the words "doom," "destined," and "fated" so often because the fixed point of its attention was a moment just before beginning, a moment that could be called the collapse of pre-history. Parkman in his Preface to *The Conspiracy of Pontiac* defined the "moment" of his history in these terms.

> Could the French have maintained their ground, the ruin of the Indian tribes might have been postponed; but the victory of Quebec was the signal of their [the Indian tribes'] swift decline. Thenceforth they were destined to melt and vanish before the advancing waves of Anglo-American power, which now rolled westward unchecked and unopposed. They saw the dangers, and led by a great and daring champion, struggled fiercely to avert it.[4]

In other words, his history is based in a moment, 1763, a little more than a decade before the formal beginning of national identity, when the last opponents, seeing their destiny clearly at last, rose up to oppose it. Since it was manifest, it was also too late for opposition. In effect, Parkman's story is the detailed closing down of the pre-history of the United States.

Because the renaming or reimagining of beginnings as endings is so fundamental to the techniques by means of which the American nation came to moral terms with the fact of the American Indian, and at the same time is so central to the strategy of Cooper, who in *The Deerslayer* provided the key American account of the historical treatment of the Indian, I want to look for a moment at two alternative, equally significant retellings of the same pre-history. Longfellow's poem *The Song of Hiawatha*, Parkman's history *The Conspiracy of Pontiac*, and Cooper's novel *The Deerslayer* are poetic, historical, and novelistic versions of the same moral and historical configuration. Each is a pre-history of America and each designs the nation's beginning as at least partially, a stained and guilty supersession.

The Song of Hiawatha is a Virgilian Epic: an epic of civilization with a central figure who brings to his people peace, order, and the successive materials of progress. Like Aeneas, Hiawatha distills the central features of national identity, and like Aeneas, he is something of a wooden prig. Through his strength and civic spirit, the Indians gain agriculture, writing, and the power over water that results from the invention of canoes. The land is rid of primitive forces which, once tamed, become the very features of civilization. Misrule and laughter, the rule of games and chance are (characteristically for the Victorians) weeded out to make "serious" progress possible.

In the figure of Hiawatha, Longfellow condenses centuries of civilization and conquest. Yet, unlike Aeneas, whose founding acts prepare for the great Roman civilization that will last for centuries, Hiawatha builds peace and order, only in his own lifetime to see the arrival of the first white missionaries with a civilization that will supersede his own and make his people wards.

After building from strength to strength, the epic of Hiawatha begins to catalogue a series of deaths and losses until, in the final book, Hiawatha himself "goes west," departing as soon as the white man arrives. His death is built into the arrival of the new masters. In the same way he had vanquished each of the previous forces. Unlike Virgil's Aeneas, the great unfolding of Hiawatha's march to conquest permits nothing but his people's extinction. Significantly, Hiawatha has no children; by the epic's end famine occurs in the land for which the coming of maize and agriculture should have eliminated the feast-and-famine cycle of the hunt. The farewell of Hiawatha begins mystically. Nature accepts his fate just as he does. However, the final verb inserts a more desperate mood.

> And the people from the margin
> Watched him floating, rising, sinking,
> Till the birch canoe seemed lifted
> High into that sea of splendor,
> Till it sank into the vapors
> Like the new moon slowly, slowly
> Sinking in the purple distance.
>   And they said, "Farewell forever!"
> Said, "Farewell, O Hiawatha!"
> And the forests, dark and lonely,
> Moved through all their depths of darkness,
> Sighed, "Farewell, O Hiawatha!"
> And the waves upon the margin
> Rising, rippling on the pebbles,
> Sobbed, "Farewell, O Hiawatha!"
> And the heron, the Shuh-shuh-gah,
> From her haunts among the fen-lands,
> *Screamed*, "Farewell, O Hiawatha!"[5]

Longfellow's narrative is end-directed, like the stories of Cooper and Parkman. It is poised at what we might call the closing down of a pre-history. In the 1840s Thomas Cole painted his "Expulsion From The Garden of Eden," a striking, reversed parable of American beginnings within the land. The new heaven, new earth, the second Adam is once again drawn out, ashamed and guilty to begin his history. The story of Eden plays the same part in the Judeo-Christian history of the world as the Indian pre-history of Longfellow, Cooper, and Parkman does for the American history that follows. Both stories describe a world in which the complete cycle has already been run and of which no traces remain. But the significance of such a pre-history as the Garden of Eden or the Song of Hiawatha is not that the traces of it remain, but rather that only such an erased story can account for the bitter taste of the history that follows. Cole's "Expulsion From The Garden of Eden," unlike Masaccio's Renaissance masterpiece, has no psychological account to give. Its subject is the world, a world almost more grand and inviting than any small-scale Eden no matter what its "features." Nonetheless the story of Eden and a painting such as Cole's provide a way of implying a tragic element to the act of beginning, in this case the beginning of civilization and human culture. No matter how great this promise, and the "world" into which Cole's pair has been banished is still a paradise of grandeur and possibility, all worlds with such pre-histories are denied the moral clarity of a clean slate from which to start. They start their story already damaged in spirit by what has had to be destroyed to make even the appropriation of this paradise or this sublime history possible. This is a history into which they have been ejected.

In this sense, Thoreau's *Walden* can be seen as a later, literal return to the pre-history but with the one morally damaging condition removed. The land is now truly empty. It does not require being "cleared" before the first founding acts can begin. In miniature, since his few acres sum up the whole of America and he can be the "first" man there, Thoreau can rewrite an expurgated pre-history that subtracts the tragic facts that taint the history that follows. *The Song of Hiawatha*, and Cooper's *The Deerslayer*, both usually seen as escapist and candied "popular" myths that leave out all of the hard facts, are in reality based on a single dark premise—that American culture is a successor culture that founds itself by extinguishing the culture already in place. This single premise, in the carefully staged national parable of Thoreau, is neatly evaded as on July 4, Thoreau sets out into the unpre-empted woods.

By an interesting contrast, Rousseau in his *Émile* of nearly one hundred years earlier, sets out with his young "savage," Émile, to teach him agriculture, or so Émile presumes. They stake out some empty land, set in their plants, and begin to water and care for them, looking forward to Émile's first harvest. One morning they come and find their garden pulled out and razed to the ground. They sound the alarm and search for the monster who could destroy so many hopes and so many hours of labor. It was the gardener Robert who tells them boldly: You planted on my land and violated my property. I tore it out to regain what was mine and plant my garden. The teacher now reveals his lesson: what he had wanted to teach his pupil were not the rules of agriculture but the laws of private property, and the first law of private property is a simple one. There is no such thing as "empty" land.[6]

Thoreau, unlike Cooper and Parkman, and even Longfellow, is able to set out into empty land. The land for Cooper or Longfellow must first be emptied. Any history must begin with the damaged purity of the now-emptied land.

Robert Frost in his poem "Spring Pools" exactly described the history of beginnings damaged by violence.

SPRING POOLS

These pools that, though in forests, still reflect
The total sky almost without defect,
And like the flowers beside them, chill and shiver,

Will like the flowers beside them soon be gone,
And yet not out by any brook or river,
But up by roots to bring dark foliage on.

The trees that have it in their pent-up buds
To darken nature and be summer woods—
Let them think twice before they use their powers
To blot out and drink up and sweep away
These flowery waters and these watery flowers
From snow that melted only yesterday.[7]

In the pattern of American founding described by Cooper, Parkman, and Longfellow, the fragile, balanced, but short-lived mutual stage of "flowery waters and watery flowers," after winter but before the force of summer, is the Indian stage. Tocqueville concludes his first chapter with an account of this same short-lived betweenness. "[The Indians] seem to have been placed by Providence amid the riches of the new world only to enjoy them for a season; they were there merely to wait till others came."[8]

The historical tough-mindedness of Tocqueville's phrase, "They were there merely to wait till others came," has its most complex historical elaboration in Parkman's *The Conspiracy of Pontiac*. Like *The Song of Hiawatha*, Parkman's first great history, appearing in 1851, four years before Longfellow's poem, is an end-structured narrative of the final legitimate moment of Indian nationhood. The moment treated by Parkman, 1763, lies a little more than ten years before the American Declaration of Independence. Parkman's moment just before American nationhood is, at the same time, the moment of a counter-attempt at genuine national Indian identity under the leadership of Pontiac who is, in effect, a failed George Washington for a possible, but now canceled Indian nation. With the defeat of the French, whose allies the Indians (as independent nations) had been during the French and English wars, the Indian Nations were now on their own without an external central figure, the French king. Could Pontiac unite them against the English and their settlers, the putative Indian nationhood could be realized. However, with Pontiac's failure, the long-term future is set. The Indians instead of unification will face atomization. Eventually they will be deprived of their stature as "nations" and will become by the 1850s Indians, the generic term that abolishes their separate cultures and structures, forcing them to deal with the American government as one more variety of troublesome individual citizens.

With the end of Pontiac's revolt and the formal peace treaty with the French, the way was clear for the future, singular sovereignty of the United States of America. The great pathos and historical power of Parkman's narrative results from his inversion of causes. He, like Cooper, picks out a unique moment of reversal in which all that is genuinely tragic in the Indian's fate can appear to be self-caused. Parkman writes at a moment of a collapse of differences. By 1850 Creeks and Delawares, Iroquois and Cherokee, Moravian converts and wild Apaches have been redesignated and flattened into "Indians." Parkman looks back to a moment in which the Indians themselves under Pontiac had reached up for a higher common purpose that likewise would have had to abolish differences.

There are many small tragedies that Parkman describes, such as the Pennsylvania massacres of long-peaceful groups by the enraged whites who had become "Indian-killers" pure and simple, and who made no distinction between men and women, adults and children, civilized and wild. The Moravian converts, whom the Quakers attempted to protect by holding them in jail, marching them to New Jersey, and then marching them back, are only the most moving of these victims.[9] Earlier these converts had been trapped between French and English armies and their allies and were suspected by both.

> These unhappy neutrals, between the French and Indians on the one side, and the English on the other, excited the enmity of both; and while from the west they were threatened by the hatchets of their own countrymen, they were menaced on the

east by the no less formidable vengeance of the west settlers, who, in their distress and terror, never doubted that the Moravian converts were in league with the enemy. The popular rage against them at length grew so furious that their destruction was resolved upon. The settlers assembled and advanced against the Moravian community of Gnadenhutten; but the French and Indians gained the first blow, and, descending upon the doomed settlement, utterly destroyed it. This disaster, deplorable as it was in itself, proved the safety of the other Moravian settlements, by making it fully apparent that their inhabitants were not in league with the enemy. They were suffered to remain unmolested for several years; but with the murders that ushered in Pontiac's war, in 1763, the former suspicion revived, and the expediency of destroying the Moravian Indians was openly debated.[10]

The peaceful, Christianized Moravian Indians had done the maximum in order to be permitted to live under tolerance within a white civilization on land to which they had surrendered all claims. In capsule form, their situation (suspected and hunted down anyway once all categories had simplified and they were taken by the Indian killers to be just what they were—"Indians") stood for the historical fact that under any irritant they would be blamed anyway, by someone, no matter how improbable the accusation. By representing this collapse of difference as a consequence of the "murders that ushered in Pontiac's war, in 1863," Parkman is able to make the terror and reaction of the whites legitimate.

But as he himself acknowledges, the standard first step was almost always taken by the whites who had a long-term interest in this collapse of categories that for the Indians could only lead to reservations and extermination once they were "just Indians." Here is Parkman's candid description of the troubles of 1767.

With the succeeding spring, 1767, fresh murmurings of discontent arose among the Indian tribes, from the lakes to the

Potomac, the first precursors of the disorders which, a few
years later, ripened into a brief but bloody war along the
borders of Virginia. These threatening symptoms might easily
be traced to their source. The incorrigible frontiersmen had
again let loose their murdering propensities; and a multitude of
squatters had built their cabins on Indian lands, beyond the
limits of Pennsylvania, adding insult to aggression, and sparing
neither oaths, curses, nor any form of abuse and maltreatment
against the rightful owners of the soil.[11]

That the "savages on the warpath" and the "rightful owners of
the soil" were one and the same, the former occurring only as
a result of injury to the latter, Parkman here acknowledges.

Most importantly, the refusal to differentiate among the
Indians (even to the point of ridiculing the chiefs' common
claim that, while they themselves were peaceful, they had been
drawn into war by the hot-headed actions of young braves
whom they could not restrain) coexists with a very careful
differentiation of whites into murderous frontiersmen, squatters, peaceful Quakers, reasonable settlers, and so on. The
subdivisions permit moral excuses. The actions of the lawless
squatters nonetheless lead, again and again, after a period of
provocation and Indian retaliation, of white escalation and
further Indian response, to a moment when the entire white
community, with its massacring army, ratifies the initial lawless acts of the squatters, since they have now become obscured
by the later killing of innocents on all sides.

The provisions of subcategories for one side and their
collapse for the other, is one of the most far-reaching political
acts of narrative since it controls the issue of collective
responsibility or innocence and legitimizes violence on an
indiscriminate basis. It is in fact the inner mechanism by
which "justice" and the punishment of individual offenders
spreads out, under a collapse of differences, into extermination.

2. COOPER AND THE MOMENT OF 1840

In calling his novel *The Deerslayer* Cooper deflects attention from and disguises his central subject. Like the "anger" of Achilles or the "return" of Odysseus, Cooper's novel has a simple, blunt subject: the reluctant but inevitable extermination of the American Indian.[12]

The titles of Cooper's four earlier Leatherstocking Tales— *The Pioneers, The Last of the Mohicans, The Prairie, The Pathfinder*—acted as lenses that brought into focus one central realm of value. Each title neatly carved out the core fact of the book. *The Prairie* factored out the land itself over against every variety of settler, nomad, woodsman, or Indian. *The Pathfinder* (individual) and *The Pioneers* (plural) named stages of the fixed progress of white civilization, each of which defined itself against earlier or later stages with their alternate, but at this moment inappropriate, values, like those of the hunter Bumppo within the settlement of *The Pioneers*. The third antagonist to the land itself and to the white settlers in their carefully subdivided stages of civilization, is named in *The Last of the Mohicans:* the Indian, given moral reality and central position only in the act of being canceled by extinction, not *The Mohicans* but the *last* of the Mohicans.

In the final novel of his sequence Cooper's title swerves away from direct announcement of its central matter. Man is named a "slayer" in the title, but a slayer of deer. The one thing not killed in the novel is a deer. The name "Deerslayer" is one of a long list of his earlier names that Natty Bumppo gives Hetty when she asks what to her simple mind is a simple question: "What is your name?" He answers in a page-long explanation that boils down to the list: "Bumppo," "Nathaniel," "Natty," "Straight-tongue," "Pigeon," "Lap-ear," "Deerslayer." The name "Deerslayer" has already been superseded by the time the action of the novel has begun. Bumppo has killed his first man and earned the more predatory name "Hawkeye."

Within the novel itself the name "Deerslayer," falling free of the man is transferred to his rifle "Kill-deer," the gift that he received from Judith Hutter. In the chapter where he accepts this gift that will be a permanent part of himself, he turns down her other gift, herself, and refuses to join her in marriage. The rifle "Kill-deer," once accepted, and the gift of marriage refused, the phrase "Deerslayer" positions itself halfway (and by negation in both cases) between Cooper's twin subjects: massacre and marriage, extermination and reproduction. The title of this final Leatherstocking novel is the name of a gun. What is brought into focus is murderousness itself.

In his final Leatherstocking Tale, Cooper goes back in time to the earliest stage of his hero's life, the arrival at identity and name. At the same time Cooper invents the earliest and most troubling stage of the national history for which the hero's life is a surrogate. In Bumppo the transition from boy to man, from hunter to warrior, from killing deer to killing men occurs within a miniature drama of national progression from hunting and "floating" on the land to preparing for settlement by "clearing the land," that is, wiping out the Indians. Cooper writes *The Deerslayer* in 1840 at the moment of the conclusion of the Jacksonian Indian Removal: this policy had cleared the states east of the Mississippi of significant Indian presence and set up the barrier of an Indian territory west of the Mississippi filled with resettled and demoralized remnants of the Five Tribes, expelled from the Southeast.[13] The Jacksonian policy of resettlement led, of course, to the ultimate resettlement onto reservation lands, as white land hunger ate into the Indians' territory over the next fifty years. What had been effected east of the Mississippi by 1840 previewed the future Indian solution for the continent as a whole. Cooper writes, in other words, at the moment when the outline of the national solution was in place, and at the moment when the first cycle of Indian wars and removal had already been completed for the Eastern states. The states were finally sovereign over all of their territory and "cleared" of the Indian nations even where isolated Indian pockets remained.

By 1838 the Cherokees had been removed from Georgia and completed their trek to the newly assigned territories west of the Mississippi. Like every sweeping policy, Indian removal had, in dealing with the Cherokees and the state of Georgia, reached what lawyers refer to as its "hard" case. Absolute laws—the existence of the death penalty, the absence of a death penalty—satisfy in the middle for the average cases for which they were designed, but then encounter paradoxical, unpredictable complications of circumstances that make, on the one hand, execution, or on the other, being forbidden to execute, a public outrage. Just as every policy has its own range of average and foreseen applications quite different from the profile for any alternate policy, so too does each have its own paradoxical hard cases and outrageous instances in which what started out as justice finally appears an even worse form of injustice than lawlessness itself. And every policy unfolds to meet, finally, this set of antagonists for which it has no accurate description and in the face of which it becomes clumsy and outrageous to any spontaneous, common sense notion of fairness.

The Cherokees had taken up farming, learned to read and write, adopted a peaceful and settled life, but found themselves facing a collapse of categories, a historical moment in which there were no longer good-Indians and bad-Indians, farming versus hunting, settled versus migratory, Christianized versus "wild," literate versus illiterate, civilized versus savage, peaceful versus warlike. All of the categories of classification and ranking that had been nurtured by one group or another for two hundred years so as to make some part of the Indian world acceptable to some part of the white world had disappeared, and by the Jacksonian Indian Removal Policy the land east of the Mississippi was to be cleared of everything falling into the single remaining category: Indians.

On the Oregon Trail, that had within a ten-year period permitted massive crossings by settlers through the supposedly inviolate territories onto which the Indians had been resettled, Francis Parkman described the scene of juncture between Indian and white in 1846:

> Warriors, women and children swarmed like bees; hundreds of dogs, of all sizes and colors ran restlessly about; and, close at hand, the wide shallow stream was alive with boys, girls, and young squaws, splashing, screaming and laughing in the water. At the same time a long train of emigrants with their heavy wagons was crossing the creek, and dragging on in slow procession by the encampment of the people whom they and their descendents, in the space of a century, are to sweep from the face of the earth.[14]

The 1840s are the moment in which this future is unmistakably clear so that any narrative of the past takes on a fatality. This is so because within the present, the future, unsuspected by most of the actors, is already visible. Such a future, to which the general will has committed itself, makes of every small scale event a sample of a general fate and permits both a portentous tone, and an elevated feeling of necessity in plots and histories. Once the large historical action has been run through completely in miniature, the mechanisms and legalities of its later, general case are already clear and wait only for the timing. Just as the United States had by 1840 swept the Indians from the East, Parkman can see everywhere the seeds of the more general case. Shortly the white settlers will come to "sweep [them] from the face of earth."

The combination of, on the one hand, the political end point of Jacksonian Indian Removal Policy that cleared the East, and, on the other, the climax of historical self-consciousness in the works of Bancroft, Tocqueville, and Parkman marks out the 1840s as a plateau from which the structure of the American past was suddenly unmistakable. It is from this plateau that Cooper's *The Deerslayer* was written. Cooper, writing in 1840, describes events of exactly a hundred years earlier, 1740, but those events and circumstances, by means of Cooper's choice of a frontier setting, restate the average circumstances of a still earlier time, 1640. The isolation and remoteness of Cooper's 1740 upstate New York repeat the earlier isolation of just arrived, surrounded, small pockets of fragilely established whites in a land of Indians.

The geography of Cooper's novel elaborates the historical echo. The whites are at home only on the water; the Hutter clan is restricted to ark, castle, and canoes. The whites make a number of landings and incursions, raids and invasions, but the land within the novel is Indian land. The whites at this point have no location, no base of operation, except on the water. On this water they are, as the novel names them, "floaters." Once dead they are buried in the lake and no trace will remain. Once the canoes, ark, and castle are destroyed by the natural forces of weather and seasons, they will vanish likewise. The whites in their offshore boats are defined as raiders, or, as Hutter's past suggests, pirates. By calling their bases "ark" and "castle" a strongly archaic flavor is built in, as it is in the uncomfortable suggestion that this ark is, like Noah's, a saved remnant, a miniature of the entire population that will unfold itself across the land once a true landing is possible. That Cooper does intend this meaning of ark I will attempt to show in a later section where I will describe the contents of Hutter's mysterious chest. The ark carries objects and not animals, because what will be rebuilt is not nature, as in the days of Noah, but civilization for which a seeding of things is as important as the two of every animal-kind taken on board by Noah.

In their canoes, ark, and water-fort, Cooper's whites recapitulate the moment of the not yet landed first settlers, anchored just offshore. In their incursions, raids, negotiations, captivity, and final massacres they recreate literally the initial state of white settler and Indian in America. They play the history through, in miniature, to its final act. Literally, Cooper's novel is set at the *landing of white America.*

As a writer of 1840 looking back to a random, unimportant set of events taking place in a few days in 1740, Cooper reenacts through those events the primary founding events of 1620-40. In making these choices he uses the historical novel in a classic way to superimpose a series of phases so as to bring to bear in a miniature setting the largest central forces of a now-manifest history. The first appearance of his characters is given almost as a moment of original creation. They arise from a swamp.

> Centuries of summer suns had warmed the tops of the same noble oaks and pines, sending their heats even to the tenacious roots, when voices were heard calling to each other, in the depths of a forest, of which the leafy surface lay bathed in the brilliant light of a cloudless day in June, while the trunks of the trees rose in a gloomy grandeur in the shades beneath. The calls were in different tones, evidently proceeding from two men who had lost their way, and were searching in different directions for their path. At length a shout proclaimed success, and presently *a man of gigantic mold broke out of the tangled labyrinth of a small swamp, emerging into an opening that appeared to have been formed partly by the ravages of the wind and partly by those of fire.* This little area which afforded a good view of the sky, although it was pretty well filled with dead trees, lay on the side of one of the high hills, or low mountains, into which nearly the whole surface of the adjacent country was broken.
>
> "Here is room to breathe in!" exclaimed the liberated forester as soon as he found himself under a clear sky, shaking his huge frame like a mastiff that has just escaped from a snowbank. "Hurrah! Deerslayer, here is daylight, at last, and yonder is the lake."[15] (emphasis added)

The novel opens with two men, separated and lost within nature, breaking free into a clearing. No longer lost and with their location settled, they are reunited. They triumph, and

celebrate their survival over separation and their disentangle-
ment from nature. Like the dog free of the snowbank, they are
"back in the world" precisely because they have found a
clearing, from which lake and sky can be seen and their
position known. The clearing was made by violence: the
"ravages," as Cooper calls them, of wind and fire. The opening
or clearing in which location can be known and separation
overcome is, from the start, a product of natural violence.
Cooper's novel as a whole creates the reunification in a clearing
that the opening scene predicts. Location and union are pur-
chased with the sum total of human violence expended in the
novel. Even that total is not sufficient to permit a settlement
that would make of this location a named spot on a map.

The first words spoken in the novel are words of triumphant
liberation, "Hurrah, here's room to breathe in!" These words
might be the inner, candid shout of the first landed settlers,
who on the surface pour out the expected, pious prayers of
gratitude, but within shout out the pure taste of freedom
where what was expected was the more restrained note of
"deliverance." That freedom, which we might term *refound
freedom*, is Cooper's subject, both in its nature and in its
costs. Cooper's novel creates a definition of American freedom
as the freedom of the just-released captive, a freedom pur-
chased by the massacre of the captors. Both the full energy of
this freedom and its traces of guilt are built into his profound
account of recovered freedom.

In the small opening scene of the first human appearance,
Cooper displays the method of a displaced, inner history that
is a primary history precisely because it is the one that will be
unselfconsciously recreated on thousands of small occasions
that echo the basic facts of the original situation. Hurry
Harry is literally the first man. Impetuous, clumsy, gigantic;
killing by accident; failing to marry and, therefore, failing to
continue his type: he is the true figure of brute force and
unscrupulous but stupid greed that is the essence of the first
white presence on the American scene. His is a presence long
before the first settlement.

The second man to arrive is a refined and perfected version of the first. The hunter Deerslayer represents a controlled violence. He sets limits to violence by means of a personal ethos and not through the agency of an organized society or rule of law. His necessary violence civilizes the murderousness that is random, spontaneous, and often ineffective in Hurry Harry.

The third white man to arrive is Captain Warley, who appears only at the end of the novel. He leads his troops in an ordered march with drawn bayonets to massacre the Hurons. The army is the essence of formal, deputized violence. It is systematic, legal, and impersonal. It is the social form of what in Leatherstocking was personal and ethical.

The sequence of white male appearances is only one of the features of *The Deerslayer* that, in miniature, repeat the earliest steps towards the settlements that, in their turn, lead to the colonies that resulted in the nation of 1840. The term "Ark" that Cooper uses for the boat that is the central, safe location for the whites throughout the novel suggests that this is the temporary home for those who cannot yet land. Many brief episodes of landing occur throughout the novel. Again and again the shoreline is studied from an approaching canoe to estimate what dangers it conceals. Then a first contact occurs. The primary moment of Cooper's novel is the moment just before landing and therefore, just before the beginning of white presence in America. Night landings; solitary landings; unwilling landings; like that of the drifting canoe on the bottom of which Deerslayer lies concealed; landings done to raid; landings to bring the Gospel; voluntary landings like Deerslayer's return after his furlough: the entire set of landings subdivides the emotional fact of the first, unretracted step onto the land.

All landings within the novel lead either to retraction or to captivity. The action of the novel as a whole accomplishes three things: (1) the marriage of Chingachgook and Hist; (2) the extermination of the Huron camp; (3) the retraction of the floating settlement of the Hutters and the withdrawal of all who have landed. Writing just at the time of the American push to control the entire continent, Cooper looked back to the symbolic stage just before the beginning of this process. Like Longfellow, Cole, and Parkman, Cooper wrote the end of pre-history.

3. A SURROUNDED MAN, RESCUE, FREEDOM

By means of its central, repeated acts of capture and rescue, Cooper's plot miniaturizes the early stages of national history in a compelling way. One bride, held prisoner in a camp, can be seen as a wronged and cramped figure, denied her rightful future: her chosen husband, their children and the continuity that those children would represent. So, too, the entire, frail set of early settlements within the American wilderness can be redesignated. No longer "invaders," they are "prisoners" surrounded by hostile Indians. Once visualized as prisoners or captives with their freedom limited by the surrounding hostility, and with their future uncertain (as postponed marriages symbolize), they become the victims and seem licensed to whatever violence, now seen as purely reactive, may be needed to end their captive state and recover their freedom.

The ballet of rescues and captures, ransoms, furloughs, and attempts at forced marriage, legitimatizes the violence of the whites and defines it as retaliation. The captivity plot also isolates the central American "right" of freedom as the motive for every act within the novel. The freedom that Cooper is concerned with is what John Stuart Mill called negative freedom, which is freedom *from* x, or y, or z, as opposed to positive freedom, the freedom *to do* x, or y, or z.[16]

Captivity is, in Cooper's novel, another word for being surrounded. Hutter, who has had to move to the middle of the lake after being burnt out several times, once with the loss of his son, is surrounded by water. The lake is, in its turn,

surrounded by land that is filled with Indians. Until the end of
the novel, the fundamental condition of the whites, whether
captive or free, is to be surrounded. In America all whites
were surrounded until they came, in time, to surround the
Indians whom they then squeezed onto reservations. From
the early settlements to the final reservation policy, whites
and Indians traded places. The whites began with forts, trading
posts, and isolated settlements surrounded by Indian country.
At last, by the end of the 19th century, they had come to
surround the few remaining Indian lands. Within Cooper's
novel the climax acts out this reversal. Leatherstocking and
his friends, surrounded and outnumbered, hear the approach
of the army and at that moment the Indians see that now *they*
are surrounded. "A general yell burst from the *enclosed*
Hurons" (582, emphasis added). This moment of reversal,
along with their newly enclosed state, previews their final end
on reservations.

The image of being surrounded is a fundamental psychic
picture in America: the wagons drawn up in a circle, the fort
in the wilderness, the house or barn with the enemy on all
sides. The Indians themselves, in their final decline into
messianic illusions late in the 19th century, sometimes claimed
that the whites who now surrounded them were only a small
ring of whites who were in their turn surrounded by a world
of Indians whom they—the Indians at the center—had not yet
established contact with.[17] The potency of the captivity story
lies in the fact that it registers in a schematic form the state of
the earliest settlers. One powerless figure, tied to a tree, around
whom a mob of howling and taunting figures circle as they
invent a prolonged death, symbolically enacts the first inner
model of relatively powerless and surrounded settler life.
Captivity has as its partner figure rescue, itself a complex and
differentiated act.

The entire moral range of captivity and rescue is patiently
worked out in Cooper's novel of landing. Before the novel
begins, Hist is a captive, destined to be the wife of one of her

captors. If she accepts, she will join the tribe and become a Huron. Next, Hutter and Harry are made captive, but they are criminals caught at the scene of a crime. Found in the camp on a scalping expedition, their captivity is the socially universal captivity of outlaws who will be justly punished. Hawkeye, the third captive, is the most complex case. On the surface he is a substitute prisoner, since he is captured in the very moment of freeing Hist. He takes her place. Captives are never really freed within the story. An exchange is always made, whether deliberately, as in the ransom of Harry and Hutter, or implicitly, as when Hist is freed, but Hawkeye captured. Once he has taken her place, Hawkeye is faced with the identical offer that had been put to Hist. If he will marry into the tribe he will be fully accepted. The woman that he would have to marry is the widow of the Indian that he had earlier killed in the dispute over the canoes. Further, in the middle of his ordeal, he kills the brother of this same woman, thus depriving her of the last male who might supply her with food.

In isolation, Hawkeye's two killings are just; and yet, because we are made to experience the grief, fury, and bleak future of the woman, we are thus made to see that the secondary victims of all killings are themselves always "innocent victims," and that every killing has such secondary victims in the widows or children, or even in the society at large which must restructure and replace all relations once a killing has taken place. Even killings that appear locally "justified" are unjust as soon as the real, extended set of victims are included. The death of Hetty as a bystander at the final massacre is a way of underlining, with her simple-minded goodness, the basic innocence of every secondary victim. Therefore, Hawkeye's captivity uncovers the deeper question of the legitimacy of even his apparently "correct" killings for it exposes him (and the reader) to the entire range of consequences and thus asks if, even here, some restitution is not required.

Beyond the three types of captivity represented by, first,

Hist, second, Harry and Hutter, and third, Hawkeye, there remain the less easily described, voluntary entries into the Indian camp of the two white women, Judith and Hetty. In the course of the novel each of the whites enters the Indian world on a clearly defined mission. Since the camp is, in miniature, the Indian nation, the whites are represented as always entering voluntarily. The entries act out the range of white motives in the earliest moments of colonial history. First, Hutter and Harry enter for scalps, on which a bounty will be paid. They enter for money. Second, Hawkeye enters to rescue Hist and make possible the one marriage of the novel. Third, Hetty enters almost as a visitor with her ever-present Bible. She is a version of a simple-minded missionary who enters to solve whatever complexities exist by means of the answers given in the Bible. Just as Harry and Hutter represent the rapacious, mercenary invasion of the Indian world, she stands for the spiritual mission. Yet Cooper positions her close to the violent pair and she is, in her naive way, even in love with the brawny, murderous woodsman. She is his equal, a primitive of spirituality as he is a primitive of rapacity. Judith's mission is the mirror inversion of Leather-stocking's, just as Hetty's is of Hurry Harry's. Judith comes to rescue a man from a forced marriage, but in this case to win him back for herself. Her invasion of the camp would make possible a white marriage (her own to Hawkeye) that would begin the settlement of the region.

These carefully sequenced incursions and captivities, with their shrewdly differentiated outcomes, map out the mercenary, spiritual, and social motives of the general white invasion. Of these it is neither the predatory nor the spiritual drive that is most important. Rather it is the drive to marry and to prevent other marriages, to reproduce society, and to give names that continue through time that are the central drives. Because killing is never really the killing of individuals, but the killing of husbands, fathers, fiancees, wives, sons of now-destitute parents, parents of now-orphaned children, the issue of justice can never be settled by showing that the individual victim himself threatened death and therefore deserved to die.

The words "invasion" and "raid" and "incursion" are not used by Cooper to describe the white penetration of the Indian land. Historically, what we describe as the "Discovery of America" or the "Early Explorers of America" could more accurately be named the "Invasion of America" and the "Early Invaders." This word, ironically, is reserved by Cooper for Indian acts, specifically, for the later Indian incursions into what was, by then, white territory. On the second page of his novel he writes: "All we possess of security from *invasion* and hostile violence is the growth of but little more than the time that is frequently filled by a single human life" (14). Again at the conclusion of the novel, the same reversal is used. Leatherstocking defends his choice of the life of a warrior over married life by saying, "If the young men of this region stood by and *suffered the vagabonds to overrun the land*, why, we might as well all turn Frenchers at once and give up country and kin" (602, emphasis added). Were this sentence spoken by an Indian about the whites who were beginning to *overrun* the land, and against whom violent defense was needed, it would make more sense. However, for the white to look upon himself as defending the empty land against Indian "vagabonds" who might "overrun the land" is a striking reversal of vocabulary. It is exactly such a reversal that is pervasive. Invasion converts into rescue, offense into defense, clearing the land into rescuing innocent captives, surrounding into being surrounded. Ironically, and as if to show the force of reversed vocabulary, the action of the novel sets only one goal: the successful marriage of two Indians and the symbolic continuation of their people. But this outcome can only occur by means of its opposite: the massacre of the Indian camp and therefore, symbolically, the extermination of the Indian people.

Cooper has contrived a rich interplay between what is ostensibly going on and what is factually happening before the

reader's eyes. The name applied to a narrative act jars against
the reality of that act. It is by no means either a simple
ideological distortion in which "clearing the land" is renamed
"rescuing the captives" or "making possible the marriage"
hides "massacring the Indians," nor is it a simple, radical
display of the gap between descriptions and actions. Instead,
Cooper has worked out the very essence of a tentative and
provisional border state of society. Overlapping claims and
descriptions, and the multiplied names that result, have not
yet been simplified into what we call "Proper Names."

In the final pages of the novel Judith thanks Leatherstocking
by saying, "You've done enough already in *clearing this region*
of the Hurons, since to you is principally owing the credit of
our late victory" (603). What she calls "our late victory" is the
renamed massacre, and even if the word "victory" is appropriate, it is a victory that has cleared the land of whites as well
as Indians and left behind only ruins. At the same time, she
credits Hawkeye, and not the army, with "clearing" the land
and making it safe for white marriages and settlement. On his
side, Hawkeye would describe what he has done during the
week-long action of the novel as helping Chingachgook regain his bride.

The very question of what has happened dissolves into the
border condition of descriptions. Bumppo himself is between
boy and man, between Deerslayer and Hawkeye. The world
itself is between nature and settlement, between water and
land, between peace and war, between Indian and white.
Most people as well as most actions within the novel have
several names. Hutter, as we learn from the wanted poster, is
really a man named Harvey. Hutter is an assumed name. To
the Indians he is "The Muskrat" and to Hurry Harry he is
"Floating Tom." To the Indians Judith is "The Wild Rose."
During the week in which the novel takes place, Bumppo
gains the name Hawkeye, assigned by the Indian, and Judith
loses the name "Hutter" when she discovers that Harvey
(known to her as Hutter) was not her father. Judith fails to

gain a new last name in marriage when she rejects the proposal of Hurry Harry and is in her turn rejected by Bumppo. In the final paragraph of the novel she is left nameless and described only by the mysterious words, "There was a lady of rare beauty in the lodge who had great influence over him [Sir Robert Warley], though she did not bear his name" (612).

The lake itself is known in the novel by a translation of its Indian name, "Glimmerglass," because it has not yet been named, surveyed, and included on maps as it will be in one of the later stages of settlement. When Leatherstocking first sees the lake, he uses a striking phrase about naming: "'If they've not begun to blaze the trees, and set up their compasses, and line off their maps, its likely they've not bethought them to *disturb natur' with a name*'" (44, emphasis added). After a discussion, he makes the same point even more strongly. "'I'm glad it has no name, resumed Deerslayer, 'or, at least, no paleface name, for their christenings always foretell waste and destruction'" (45). His own names—Straight-Tongue, Pigeon, Lap-Ear, Deerslayer, and Hawkeye—are successive, frozen positions of his identity. The rifle is named Kill-Deer as though to direct its aim away from human targets. When Hurry Harry speaks of the Indians, he calls them "creatures . . . that have neither souls nor names" (450). Even the abduction and rescue of Hist turns on which of two husbands, a Delaware or a Huron, she will accept, and therefore which of two tribal names. In the border state, the in-between state, that Cooper is describing, the power of names arises from the fact that names assert claims and rights. For a person, the name is the fixed residue of action that narrows attention. The name "Hawkeye" narrows Bumppo to the single trait of his perfect aim. Names are earned. The procedure of earning a name can be seen in a simple example.

After Hutter and Harry have been freed as a result of Leatherstocking's negotiations, Cooper refers to them, several hours later, with these words: "The *two ransomed prisoners* felt humbled and dishonored" (279). He has replaced their

names with the term "ransomed prisoners." He does so because
certain experiences linger on, either as a mark of honor or as a
stain, for a time after they have ended. For the rest of his life a
man may be known as an "ex-con." Just how long—two
hours? two weeks? two years?—will these two be best identified
as "ransomed prisoners"? Will the term hold long enough to
become a name, like the name "Deerslayer" which is an
experiential event (slaying a deer), converted into a temporary
term, and then outlasting any rival terms so as to harden into
a name. Even a name can be replaced by a new name when,
once he has killed a man, the name "Hawkeye" is earned.

In "ransomed prisoners" we see the shadow of events cast
by language through time. It is for that reason that rival
names go hand in hand with rival claims. A simplification of
claims results in a unique lasting name. Terms and names
such as Harvey, Hutter, The Muskrat, Deerslayer, Hawkeye,
Ransomed Prisoners are in turmoil and subject to luck and
skill. They are as open to contest as the names of places which
directly reflect rights and forms of ownership. Marriage and
true parenthood are at stake in Cooper's novel because the
relation of women to names and rival claims is a simple map
of the condition of the land.

A conversation between Hurry Harry and Leatherstocking
early in the novel makes clear the close tie of names and
claims.

"The country is claimed by both Mingos and Mohicans and
is a sort of common territory to fish and hunt through in time
of peace, though what it may become in wartime the Lord only
knows!"

"Common territory!" exclaimed Hurry, laughing aloud. "I
should like to know what Floating Tom Hutter would say to
that. He claims the lake as his own property, in virtue of fifteen
years possession, and will not be likely to give it up to either
Mingo or Delaware without a battle for it."

"And what would the Colony say to such a quarrel? All this
country must have some owner, the gentry pushing their

cravings into the wilderness, even where they never dare to
ventur', in their own person, to look at the land they own." (20)

The total of claimants is four: two Indian tribes whose overlapping use works only in peace-time; a white squatter whose
claims are based on occupation; and white gentry who, without ever having seen it or worked on it, holds pieces of paper
that give them title.

Cooper is often faulted for not having freed himself, as a
writer of adventure novels, from a core of marriage intrigues.
However, in *The Deerslayer* the marriage questions restate in
a unique and profound way the central matters of names,
competing claims, and the right to extend claims through
time. Likewise, one image of the refusal to give names or
make claims is the mobile, unmarried life of Leatherstocking
in which any claims that he did make would end with his own
life.

At the beginning of the novel the Hurons hold both the
land and the abducted bride, Hist, whom they hope will
marry one of their tribe. On both sides an unmarried woman—
Hist and Judith—is surrogate for the land. Each will take a
name, just as the land will. The restoration of the bride to her
rightful husband is the action of the novel at the marriage
level. Hist is returned to Chingachgook, and Judith, failing to
get what she wants, is restored (but without taking his name)
to Sir Robert Warley in England. She has "relapsed into her
early failing" and become the mistress of the English officer
who was her first lover. Since both Hist and Judith leave the
scene of the novel, the land itself is restored for the time being
to nameless nature.

4. KILLING A MAN, KILLING A WOMAN, KILLING THEM ALL

On one side *The Deerslayer* describes Leatherstocking's coming
to manhood and his earning of the adult name Hawkeye.
Without any qualification these steps into full adulthood

result directly from killing a man. Gaining identity can only occur in the act of depriving another of his life, and thus his identity. At the national level, since Cooper's novel takes place just thirty years before the creation of American national identity, this suggests that all such identities are not invented, but occur in the act of supressing the identity of another.

In his boyhood as a hunter, Leatherstocking moves through a world of plenty. With the first acts of settlement, claims become exclusive, unlike the rights to hunting lands that can be shared. The adult world of marriage, around which all of the killings occur, is the epitome of exclusive claims. Marriage, in that way, is like farming. Land can belong only to one if it is to be worked and made fruitful. The onset of unshareable wealth and fruitfulness is announced by killings that thin out the claimants. As a national story, Cooper's novel ties the necessity of killing to a world that can no longer be shared, as it is in hunting, but will be appropriated, as in settlements and marriages.

A carefully staged sequence of killings, each more socially destructive than the one before, marks off the progress of *The Deerslayer* and factors out the separate components of Indian killing. In the first action of the novel, the entire Chapter 7 offers a step-by-step account of Leatherstocking's first killing. In this act he earns the name Hawkeye from his generous, dying victim. Next, at the very center of the novel, where women, marriage proposals, and the rescue of Chingachgook's bride, Hist, dominate the flow of events, the senseless killing of a young woman occurs. The slaying of the Indian girl, while on her way to a rendezvous with her lover, isolates a more disturbing murder for analysis. Finally, in the last chapters, the massacre of men, women, and children at bayonet point concludes the novel. Here we reach the third and most fundamental of the acts of Indian killing: the extermination of a society.

The three killings that Cooper has isolated map out the three fundamental facts of civilization and make the killing of

Indians incidental, but inevitable, to each of them. The first is
a killing over disputed property. The second is a killing within
the tangle of courtships and marriage possibilities. It is, therefore, a killing over who will reproduce and thus make permanent the claims and names that each has asserted. The
third is a massacre that clears the land of all overlapping
claims. Property, reproduction, and the clearing of the land
are the three territories in which killing and, along with
killing, maturing, occur.

Killing A Man: Property. The primal quarrel of American
history is the ever-shifting battle between white settlers and
Indians over the white claims to the land that they found
already peopled by the Indians. Whether the form is Papal
Decree or Royal Grant, purchase by the Dutch or treaties and
thefts, the "self-help" of squatters or the acts of legalistic
paper holders, the quarrel is always over the Indians' land and
the white man's claims. Leatherstocking's first killing reverses
this primal quarrel. At the same time it displays the intellectual core of the sophistry that governed all white analysis
of the property quarrel. By inversion, Leatherstocking kills
the Indian in a quarrel over what is unmistakably *white*
property and dubious Indian claims to it. They quarrel over
two canoes.

The world of water is the white geography of the novel.
Ark, castle, and three canoes (one object for each of the five
white characters): these five offshore objects, with their contents, define what is white property. The settlers have their
fort in the middle of the lake and their graveyard as well. The
land, forest, clearings, and camp are in Indian hands. Every
white approach to the land occurs in the form of a raid or a
mission.

In the dispute over the canoes, Bumppo, after being fired
upon from ambush, gets the drop on the Indian. The latter
agrees to settle the matter peacefully by inspecting the canoes.
The workmanship will tell whether Indian or white owns the
property. Both men agree that the two canoes show traces of

white workmanship. Here Cooper retraces the common white settler argument that only work and improvement confer ownership, never simply prior use. The land does not belong to the Indians simply because they were there first. Because the Indian hunted over the land and did not settle down, build, and improve the land, it could not be said to be his. Only he who converts land into farms, and wilderness into settlements owns anything at all. The conclusion of the first chapter of Tocqueville's *Democracy in America* makes this point in a typical way.

> Although the vast country that I have been describing was inhabited by many indigenous tribes, it may justly be said, at the time of its discovery by Europeans, to have formed one great desert. The Indians *occupied without possessing it.* It is by agricultural labor that man appropriates the soil, and the early inhabitants of North America lived by the produce of the chase. Their implacable prejudices, their uncontrollable passions, their vices, and still more, their virtues, consigned them to inevitable decay. The ruin of these tribes began from the day when Europeans landed on their shores; it has proceeded ever since, and we are now witnessing its completion.[18] (Emphasis added)

That Tocqueville proceeds so rapidly from denying Indian property rights to a tough-minded progressive report on their inevitable destruction shows that Cooper's link between the property argument (identical to Tocqueville's in its Lockean emphasis on work) and killing is radically correct. To lose this argument is to lose the right to exist.

After conceding the white man's right to both canoes, the Indian turns away. Then, with no standing point left, he fires from ambush. Hawkeye, who fires only to save himself now that every reasonable alternative is gone, kills the Indian. In each of his killings, or in the killings that occur because of Leatherstocking, the primary issue is, at the critical moment, pushed aside. He acts reluctantly to save his own life. We are asked to look at it and see that he "saved himself" rather than "killed a man." His killings are self-rescues. But the core of the dispute remains active even though shunted aside in the moment of killing. After Deerslayer has been named Hawkeye by his dying opponent, he returns to his canoes and finds that one of them is, once again, being claimed by an Indian. This time his threat is enough to get the Indian to abandon his claim. With this small reminder of the central matter, the chapter ends. Manhood, identity, property, and killing have been woven together around unshareable wealth, for which a bride is the novel's central image, and a canoe its local symbol in Leatherstocking's first killing. Both canoe and bride are tokens of the murderous quarrel over the land itself.[19]

The kinds of property that exist within the novel are revealing. Land itself is not in question, since the historical moment is prior to settlement, prior even, in symbolic terms, to an irrevocable landing. The first layer of property is that of equipment or gear, and includes canoes, rifles and, in addition, what are the only true objects in Tocqueville's sense, the ark and the carefully built castle. In these objects of use, Hutter's work and skill have appropriated nature and created property. The second form of property is persons, chiefly women, who can be stolen, won in courtship, recaptured. By offering bounty payments, the colony has also converted the Indians into objects of wealth. Every man, woman, and child, once dead, is worth so much to the killer. The bounty system raises killing to a wealth-creating act. Finally, the concept of property is symbolized most powerfully by the chest of stolen goods that Hutter owns and that his daughters will inherit. The chest is only opened once violence and stealth are transcended in the first civilized act between white and Indian: the ransom negotiations that will free Hutter and Harry. The mutual world of giving one's word and keeping it, finding possible values that can be exchanged so that violence may be avoided, accepting diplomacy and the exchange of prisoners, all preview a future stage of more peaceful relations. It is in order to find something worth exchanging that the chest is broken open and searched. In a condensed form the chest, with its costumes, games, instruments, and pistols, previews the entire civilization that will, in the long run, be set in place by the whites. Since the objects within the chest are tokens of the processes that transcend killings, I will postpone my analysis of them until the next section.

Because Hutter was a pirate, this chest of goods, the essential white wealth, is stolen property. Proudhon's famous phrase "Property is Theft!" is literally true of the chest and the civilization that Hutter and his family have brought. As we learn from documents in the chest, even his daughters are not his own, nor is his name. That the whites live off the fruits of piracy suggests that their future possession of the Indian land will be a similar tainted act.

Killing A Woman: Reproduction. The struggle over women is closely linked to the question of property. Women can be stolen, as Hist has been, thus setting in motion the action of the novel. The prominence of rivals calls up the propertylike deprivation that the exclusive rights of marriage entail. Harry and Hawkeye are rivals for Judith, even though one of them is an unconscious rival of the other. Chingachgook and the Huron youth are rivals for Hist. Marriage is also externally connected to property. At the end of the novel the Hutter family's claim to Glimmerglass must be abandoned if Hawkeye will not marry Judith and settle there to continue the claim. In fact, without a successful marriage, property becomes ruins, as the ark, castle, and canoes have by the final pages of the novel.

Killings that took place among men, but over women, would not be different from the killing over the canoes. The killing of a woman is entirely different because, like the refusal to marry, it wipes out the future. In some ways the essence of a bounty payment for scalps is the encouragement and legitimacy that it gives to the killing of women and children. Adult males can be killed in battle, and even lured into battle, but their loss is only a temporary one. By killing women the race itself is at risk since the warriors cannot be replaced.

If we look back for a moment to the larger national picture, the whites needed not only to make claims but also to make good those claims. They needed not only to claim the land but to populate it and work it in order to hold it. In fact, however worthless the settlers' claims from a legalistic point of view, the fundamental success of the Anglo-American settlements depended on the speed with which the land was flooded with population.[20] The French, for example, no matter how valid their claims, failed utterly to populate their territories. Again and again, down to the question of Texas or the Oregon Territories, American success resulted from the flood of population.

In Cooper's novel, the failure of any of the whites to marry is decisive. The erotic circularity is suicidal for the group. Harry wants to marry Judith, who rejects him because she has come to love Leatherstocking, who rejects her. Hurry Harry was loved by Hetty, but she is too simple-minded. Hawkeye's choice not to marry, with which the novel ends, is linked to his refusal to settle and his implicit refusal to continue the Hutter claims.

The refusal to marry has the same effect as the killing of marriageable women. In the most senseless killing of the novel, Harry shoots at an Indian guard and hits instead the young woman who has come to rendezvous with him. As if to match this killing exactly, Hetty is later killed in the massacre, also accidentally. The killing of both women is incidental, inadvertant, and both result from indiscriminant violence, the first associated with bounty hunting and the second with an army operation. Since Harry kills the young woman "by accident" while on his way to scalp and claim bounty payments by killing whatever sleeping Indians he happens to find in the camp, we might ask what difference there is between this accidental killing and the bounty killings that would have taken place had he been able to land. Both involve the killing of innocent victims. Both involve women and children as objects. In the case of the wild shot that brings down the Indian girl, there is the simple difference that Harry will not be able to collect payment since he cannot scalp her after shooting her down.

The breaking of Indian marriages is the primary visible consequence of almost every white act that we see in the novel. After Hawkeye has been captured, we see the widow of the Indian that he killed in the quarrel over the canoes. With no one to provide for her she is even willing to marry the killer of her husband. The killing of the Indian girl by Harry breaks off her courtship and leaves the guard without a mate. Even the recovery of Hist leaves the young Huron, who had hoped to marry her, deprived of a mate. The many unaccomplished marriages thin out the future in advance.

Hetty and the Indian girl die from undirected violence which on the frontier takes two forms. First, violence accompanies the impulsive, greed of Harry and Hutter. Second, undirected and impersonal violence follows from the formal and legalized actions of the soldiers. Hutter and Harry are outside the law. At the first sight of the noble stag in Chapter 3, Harry instinctively raises his rifle and fires. After being ransomed, he and Hutter grab for their guns to fire at the backs of the Indians who have just carried out an honorable agreement and freed them. They raid the camp for scalps. As one component of their rapacity, Cooper installs a haste that usually misses its aim. They fail in their raid; the shot misses the deer; and, firing at the guard, Harry instead hits the girl. The accuracy of Deerslayer's violence comes from the curbing of violence by thought and intention. His is the minimized, deliberate violence of a higher stage, one that will replace the sprayed bullets of the outlaws.

Cooper, however, makes Leatherstocking only a transitional figure. He stands between the lawless, random violence of the Harrys and the Hutters and the even more deadly indiscriminate violence of the army that marches in to clear out the Indians. Now legal, the violence has better aim, but it aims at everyone.

The second killing of a young woman occurs at the hands of the army when Hetty falls amid the Indian women and children during the massacre. As has already been mentioned, the deepest irony of Cooper's plot is that its motivating center is the recovery of Hist that will make possible an ideally suited Indian marriage and the continuity that such a marriage represents. The price of this is a sequence of events that includes an Indian massacre. The price of this one token marriage is the deeper elimination of the very social frame within which this marriage might be more than an individual event.

Killing Them All: Ruins. The military massacre that concludes *The Deerslayer* is left undescribed. It is covered by the sort of narrative ellipsis usually used for sexual moments in the novel.[21] After courtship and with all obstacles overcome, the door closes, the chapter ends and the next chapter resumes what we call "coverage" some hours or days later. The ellipsis, or blank page, is there for undescribable acts. The great ellipses of the 19th-century novel—like the marriages and the first stages of married life of Isabel Archer in *The Portrait of a Lady* and Dorothea Brooke in *Middlemarch*—are unusually charged, even repellent blanks. Between the final words of Chapter 30 and the first words of Chapter 31 of *The Deerslayer* a similarly climactic ellipsis defies representation. But it is a massacre rather than a marriage. The massacre is staged, nominally, as a necessary desperate measure now that Hutter is dead, Harry gone, and Leatherstocking captured, thus leaving the white women unprotected and unable to defend their property or their lives. The massacre is also designed into the plot as a collective punishment for collective violence. Just as the individual killings done by Deerslayer react to individual threats to his own life so that we can say that he "saved himself" rather than "killed a man," so too it is only after the torture in which the entire village participates and chooses by means of councils and decisions at every stage, thereby incurring reprisal as a group, and only to prevent the communally imposed slow death that is now inevitable, that the massacre takes place, absolved in advance as "reprisal" or "saving Deerslayer's life." Because women took a prominent part in the decision to kill him and took part in the tortures they, too, are now reasonable victims.

The definition of killing as an act brought about by its victim is conspicuous in the earlier argument over the canoes and in the massacre, but it is physically represented best in the second of Deerslayer's killings, the tomahawking of the Indian called the Panther. In a rage, and violating even the clear wishes of his tribe, who plan a prolonged ordeal for Leatherstocking, the Panther throws a tomahawk aimed to split the skull of the captive and kill him at once. Hawkeye grabs the weapon that is spinning towards him. Its momentum pulls his arm back, and, almost as an automatic continuation of the motion he rethrows it, splitting the skull of his intended murderer. The split-second, continuous motion from the Indian's hand, in a circle and back, splitting his own head makes of Hawkeye almost an intermediary or bystander in the Indian's killing of himself. No time for choice or moral debate is permitted Hawkeye. There is no time to decide to kill or even to want to kill. The act becomes a clean, purely muscular, reflexive event. There is no responsibility because in the second of unexpected, automatic action there is no investment of the self in the event, even in the interval of revenge. The event seems to go on around him, like a boomerang that passes nearby on its arc. This killing is a paradigm of the exculpation that makes the Indians their own killers in each of the deliberate killings within the novel.

The arrival of the army is preceded by a cartoonlike parade of rescuers who enter the camp during the torture of Leatherstocking. One suggestion is that the massacre only occurs after the Indians have rejected every symbolic solution offered. Hetty arrives with her Bible, but Christianity fails. Judith arrives in the costume of a great lady with "orders" from the king overseas. The masquerade of civilization fails. Hist and Chingachgook arrive with rifles and theirs is the most realistic because most violent rescue attempt. But as three against so many, they stand surrounded and likely, now that they have all voluntarily entered the Indian camp, to be wiped out. But at the moment when the massacre of the small contingent around Deerslayer is about to begin, the supervening massacre of the surrounded Indians takes place. One important feature of Cooper's plot is that it has both a conscious goal (the recovery of Hist and her marriage to Chingachgook) and a latent, more sweeping goal that is simultaneously reached (the massacre).

5. BREAKING OPEN, RECLOSING, AND CARRYING AWAY THE BOX OF CIVILIZATION

If the first step of Leatherstocking's climb to maturity is the killing of a man, the second is a significant preview of the transcending of killing. Rather than free the captured whites, Hutter and Harry, by a raid on the camp that would only express once again the warriors' skills of stealth and violence, Leatherstocking negotiates their release. Force is replaced by the skills of reason, language, patience, the accommodation of the interests of both sides, and the capacity to imagine exactly what would have significant value in the mind of the opponent. The act of ransom goes beyond killing in that it replaces a crude version of exchange (achieving an identity by suppressing the identity of an opponent) with an act of exchange that acknowledges simultaneous rights, including the right of all parties to continue existing. A ransom is a bargain in which each side must *give up* possessions. It is the core of peaceful relations based on concessive solutions.

It is important to note that the whites never hold Indians prisoner in Cooper's novel. The Indians, for their part, are defined completely from beginning to end by the prisoner or set of prisoners that they hold at the moment. Hist, who has been stolen, must be stolen back, not ransomed. Hutter and Harry, who are prisoners held because of crimes they intended to commit, must be ransomed, because to steal them back would be to refuse to acknowledge their guilt and the Indians' moral right to punish them. The most important prisoner, Hawkeye, who refuses to atone, by marrying the widow, for the social consequences of his individually blameless acts, can only be freed by a massacre that dissolves the society within which those social consequences have meaning, but for which there is no answer. Ransom and massacre, unlike the raid that steals back the innocent Hist, both acknowledge responsibility to the claims of another group, but the second does so when, paradoxically, those claims can only be acknowledged by erasing the entire social order in which they can be recorded.

The Indians hold prisoners continually throughout *The Deerslayer* precisely because the first state of the white settlers in America was the state of being surrounded. To be surrounded, unable confidently to move out freely into space and time, is to be a prisoner. Moving outward in space is done by settlers and explorers; in time, by marriages and descendents. The fundamental definition that Cooper provides of American Freedom, the essential attribute of national identity, is that it is the freedom of the recently freed prisoner. Leatherstocking is by the end of the novel the quintessential American pioneer precisely because he stands, as a result of the massacre, a newly freed prisoner moving out into a cleared land.

Since ransom suggests one solution beyond massacre, the middle chapters (12 through 15) that exhaustively work out the negotiations are crucial. In these chapters the whites, to provide themselves with objects of value for which the Indians will be willing to exchange Hutter and Harry, break open Hutter's sealed chest. The overall symbolic national moment of Cooper's novel is the moment of tentative landings, the moment just before irrevocable landing takes place. The locked chest defines the whites as not yet unpacked. Like

Robinson Crusoe the arriving whites bring with them the seeds and materials that will let them plant civilization rather than slowly develop it, or rather, we might say, to graft it onto the landscape so that it is almost instantly accomplished. Since Hutter is a pirate his chest is a "treasure chest." It is both stolen and made up of pure wealth and social symbols rather than the instruments of wealth making, like the tools and nails that the box of an ordinary pioneer would contain. That the box will be reclosed and pointedly carried away at the end of the novel suggests that its artifacts are premature and must be withdrawn. The process of ransom by means of negotiations, the giving and keeping of one's word, the art of peace-making and peace-keeping are also premature and are withdrawn in the massacre. Since the women die or retreat with the chest, the suggestion exists that they, too, are here prematurely. With only Leatherstocking and Hutter left, along with the military presence offstage in case of need, the white world reverts to a small world of hunters and killers.

The contents of the chest are carefully listed and examined one by one. Each of the objects carries the narrative forward over stages of the civilizing process to the world that Cooper's readers of 1840 know to be already in place. Significantly the first object is a richly ornamented man's coat: "part of the attire of a civilian of condition at a period when social rank was rigidly respected in dress" (231). The coat imports the stratified social world with its precise sumptuary laws and it is, therefore, more a set of signals than a covering. Chingachgook immediately tries it on, propelling himself forward into a Louis XIV civilization. Cooper mocks here the "noble" savage, the French assimilation of the Indian by way of the aristocratic analogy. This scene previews, in its short theatrical failure of identity, the more important failure when Judith, in an attempt to rescue Leatherstocking, puts on an equivalent costume of a lady, but is seen through at once by the Indians.

After Chingachgook's moment of dressing into the future, Judith puts on a brocade dress and steps forward, likewise previewing high civilization. At this moment one form of the

American future is in view. After the time of deerslaying and killing, settling and nation-building, the society will at last reach the ridiculous end of a nation of fops. Just as the clothes fail and are rejected, so too the next objects in the trunk, a pair of silver inlaid pistols, again appropriate for a dueling culture of fops, fail, but with nearly fatal results. Deerslayer attempts to fire one of the pistols and it explodes, endangering everyone around him. Instead of being a symbol of protection, it is, for those who use it, a greater danger than the enemy himself.

The third image of civilization is a set of mathematical instruments, surveying instruments. These are, in fact, the first tools of settlement, since ownership of land depends upon precise surveys. Looking at them, Leatherstocking sees them as greater dangers than the exploding pistols and the foppish costumes that encourage illusions that obliterate the material self. Clothes and pistols destroy only the self that uses them. The instruments will destroy the outer world, the wilderness itself.

Deerslayer comments on surveyers, "I've seen all their tools often—and wicked and heartless enough are they, for they never come into the forest but to lead the way to waste and destruction" (244). The tools indicate a scientific and materialistic civilization that appropriates, gives names, converts to property. They are the insignia of a middle-class, utilitarian world as the dueling pistols and clothing were symbols of a feudal world of pleasure and honor. Where the feudal objects project a distant American future, the surveying instruments are the tools of the first act of landing: map-making and division of the wilderness into sections of property. Where costumes convert the self into its fantasies, the instruments with one stroke make over nature into "land."

Like the pistols and clothes, the instruments are put aside as of no use for a ransom offer since they will not necessarily have value in the Indian culture. Ransom is an image of mutuality exactly because to offer something, one has to possess it because of its value in one's own world, and for it to be accepted, it has to have great value, but not necessarily for the same reason, in the opponents' world. The final objects in the trunk are objects that the reader knows at once are chess pieces, but so isolated are Leatherstocking, Judith, and Chingachgook that not one of them knows what the objects are. They speak of them at first as "idols." These small objects are the ideal images of civilization exactly because they have so many possible values. To a chess player they are pieces for his game. To a trader they are so many ounces of ivory and worth so many dollars. As figures they are "idols." To the Indians they are images of a scientific kind, describing animals they have never seen and providing exact details of their strength and size. The chess rooks are figures of elephants carrying castles. These ivory elephants which the Indians will value because they represent animals never seen in America and presumably large enough, wherever they exist, to carry entire castles, are the novel's most profound symbol of civilization. To the whites they seem "idols," then parts of a game they do not know the rules of. To the Indians they are marvels. Whatever they are, they are an image of the odd mixture of civilization: images of African animals carved in ivory (a material unknown in either England or America) carried by Englishmen to America as part of a set of pieces for one of the oldest and most rational games known to civilization.

These chess pieces are used in the ransom because the process of negotiations, keeping one's word, bargaining, and promising are the primary features of peaceful, rational civilization. Negotiations are also gamelike in their rules and in the order of events. Ransom is a game of two players, but unlike most games it is also a game of two winners, as all peaceful relations must be. In the game of ransom, violence is prevented by each side giving up property. Thus ransom short-circuits *revenge* which is the unsettled and permanently violent form of justice.

All games and contests sublimate violence while retaining opposition. They are entirely different from a world of unity or brotherhood. Rivalry, defeat, and struggle are retained, but with the ending removed. Games and contests, historically, are the inverse of the practice or previews that precede climactic situations. Games are the aftermath, the tracing, and retracing after the event of battles that now can end without losses. This is one way of suggesting why the single ransom within Cooper's novel does not set a pattern of peaceful negotiations. Like the clothes put on by Judith and Chingachgook, the chess piece ransom is only a glimpse forward towards a time when the furious and deadly battles about to begin (battles that were at their high point during the mid-19th century) would already be part of the past. Like the game of chess itself, which not one of Cooper's characters can play, the ransom is a distant, stable possibility.

Yet the game structure is pervasive in Cooper's novel. Even in torture the spirit of a game of rivalry that suggests the civilizing of violence is present. The Indians compete to throw a tomahawk closest to the prisoner's head *without drawing blood*. The many contests within the novel point towards alternatives to killing and extermination. Deerslayer's last act before going back to face torture is to test out his new rifle, Killdeer, in a shooting contest with Chingachgook. The novel describes a canoe race, the wrestling bout between Harry and the Indians, and a number of other moments where endurance, strength, and skill are tested, but under circumstances not yet gamelike in that to lose, here, is to die. Nonetheless, the pleasure of the contest is evoked, as it is conspicuously in the canoe race and the wrestling, as though the dangerous and ungamelike outcome could be put out of mind while the contest is in progress.

Contests and games are like marriage in Cooper's novel, markers for a more advanced state of civilization that cannot be reached without first being withdrawn for an interval of violence, as the chest, repacked, is carried away by the army for the single remaining woman. The marriages and contests, the highly abstract struggle of chess are removed until the work of violence has been accomplished.

Two attempts are made to free prisoners by using the materials of the chest. The elephants create peace when they pass from hand to hand and the prisoners are freed. The aristocratic dress that Judith puts on to "issue orders" and deceive the Indians into releasing Leatherstocking, fails completely. Civilization in the novel is not represented by a refined, class structure with ornamental symbols. The Indians recognize the simple woman, "The Wild Rose" to them, hidden within a social role. Chess piece and dress are alternative previews, but only the chess piece works. Many stages along, the civilization of contests and games, rule-structured, mutual behavior will be the aftermath of the border world of rapacity, extermination, separation, capture, and rescue that is the preliminary stage of "landing."

The small ivory images of elephants, animals none of his characters have ever seen, at the same time, parts of a game that not one of his characters has ever played, are powerful tokens of the future. In two successive chapters Cooper runs through the reactions of each of his characters, whites first, Indians second, to the mysterious objects that have brought the one act of peace. While Rivenoak and Leatherstocking negotiate, Cooper comments in an aside:

> Little did either of them imagine at the time that long ere a century elapsed, the progress of civilization would bring even much more extraordinary and rare animals into that region, as curiosities to be gazed at by the curious, and that the particular beast about which the disputes contended [ivory elephants] would be seen laving its sides and swimming in the very sheet of water on which they had met. (269–70)

Rivenoak and Leatherstocking floating on the water, negotiating, are only the first step towards the "civilized" moment in which landing and settlement will bring not only a name to the lake, but a traveling circus to the spot, so that real elephants will be washed down at the lake's shore. Like the foppish appearance of Chingachgook when he puts on the ornate coat, this glance forward to civilization itself is a painful one, since so much violence will bring only pleasures that are almost comically trivial. The ivory elephant rook does not predict a nation of chess players, but a people who will pay to see the marvels of P.T. Barnum.

In the 1840s, as pioneers moved west on the Oregon Trail the phrase "seeing the elephant" became a well-known slogan. John Unruh, who traces the phrase and its importance in his book *The Plains Across*, defines its basic meaning as having already gone through the whole experience with its trials and unexpected difficulties and managing to survive to come back and tell about it.[22] Those heading back were always questioned by the outbound pioneers: "Did you see . . .?" "Did you see . . .?" The phrase for having seen it all was "seeing the elephant." Cooper builds into his novel of landing the preview of later history provided by the trunk and its contents and, even more importantly, by the negotiations and ransom. Rivenoak and Leatherstocking, negotiating out on the water, represent the deeper white-Indian relations beneath the surface of friendship and helpfulness that the more prominent camaraderie of Leatherstocking and Chingachgook masks. In the surface plot, the white man is here only to help the Indian regain his bride, and thus to be able to reproduce and continue. But out on the water, working out the ransom of the white scalping party, Leatherstocking and Rivenoak have already "seen the elephant."

6. THE COMPOSITE WILL

The historical novel as Cooper inherits it from Scott devises a surface of what seem at first to be alternate ethical and personal styles. The truthfulness, skill, and reluctant violence of Deerslayer we see opposed to the clumsy, impulsive, rapacious, frequently failed, or randomly murderous acts of Hutter and Harry. The Christian piety of Hetty with her Bible seems one alternative to the worldy "fallen" toughness of Judith with her townlike gowns and artifices. But beneath these apparent alternatives and stylistic models open to emulation or choice, the historical situation that Cooper devises is not primarily ethical at all. That is, it is not a matter of choices that might or might not have been made and therefore of outcomes that might or might not have been brought about, and for which the agents become responsible because they could have chosen otherwise. Rather it is a sequence of interlocking acts that brings this entire range of types into a combined forward-moving plot that leads to a conclusion for which they are all somehow responsible and yet for which only their amalgamated strengths and weaknesses, stupidities and skills, virtues, and viciousness, can be cited as the *cause*. It takes *both* the nobility of Deerslayer, who returns to keep his word and face torture, and the stupidity and bad aim of Harry, who shoots down the Indian girl while aiming at the brave, to bring about, along with every other thread, the final massacre. The outcome is profoundly communal.

As a result of Lukács's classic description of Scott in *The Historical Novel*, the central invention of Scott's new form is taken to be a new kind of central hero, the bland ordinary hero, both a product and a representative figure for historical and cultural forces of the moment. Of equal importance, and in Cooper's case, of far greater importance, was Scott's invention of a plot or central action that is truly social. The outcomes are the result of a composite social will and not individual moral choice between alternatives. Intended and inadvertent consequences are complexly interwoven and often indistinguishable. The central matter becomes a nominal subject: in Cooper's case the rescue and restoration of Hist to her intended husband.

The incidental deaths, relationships, massacre, abandonment of the lake, the new name that Deerslayer earns: all occur along the margins of this simple central act. It is typical

and very significant that Deerslayer does not earn the name
Hawkeye as a part of the rescue itself, but in a self-contained,
irrelevant, subsidiary action involving the canoes, the Hutters,
the danger to the ark and castle should the Indians obtain
canoes. Similarly, the dangers to Bumppo, once he has been
captured are multiplied by the self-contained, subsidiary action
of the senseless shooting of the Indian girl by Hurry Harry.
The momentum towards a final massacre is a composite
momentum fueled by the individual and morally incompatible
"independent" decisions taken at various moments by Deerslayer, Hurry Harry, Hutter, Chingachgook, and so on.

The plot is therefore a model of a democratic, collective
result of strongly independent wills that are individually ineffective, except locally, and that find themselves subjected to
summation. Deerslayer would never choose to have his set of
choices made composite with even the separate independent
choices of Chingachgook, who, for his part, *does* set out on a
scalping party that will have consequences for any later predicament that Deerslayer may find himself in.

The configurations brought about by a series of interfering
moral patterns, local results chosen under one set of values
that are then factored into other results arrived at by opposite
moral choices, represent the overall action as the product of a
composite social will to whose unpredictable and unwilled
(considered from the point of view of the individual) consequences each will find himself subject. Gentle farm families,
even Quakers, may come to settle here and "benefit" from the
cleared land that the murderous acts of Hutter and Harry
have, in part, brought about.

The consequences, both benefits and reprisals, will fall,
unearned, on the society as a whole, or on some set of its
members. The fabric is made of small-scale individual decisions, such as Judith's decision to attempt a rescue of Hawkeye
by dressing in the costume of a grand lady, or Harry's decision
to leave after his proposal has been rejected by Judith—a
decision to leave that brings back the cavalry to massacre the

Indians and "rescue" Hawkeye—or Harry's decision to fire at
the Indian and, given his impulsive bad aim, cut down the
Indian girl standing nearby. Even the "misses" are summed in
as "hits," but hits of unintended targets. What Cooper is able
to achieve with this plot based on a composite social will is the
miniaturization, within a small group, of the nature of action
within society at large. Such a plot has two important results.
First, it makes more complex the relation of individual moral
responsibility to composite outcomes. Each one participates,
but who, really, has *caused* this outcome? Secondly, the consequences of specialization within composite actions appear
on the moral plane.

With the Indians, as Cooper elegantly shows in the structure
of his action, the same specialization has taken place. The
murderous and clumsy frontiersmen willing to kill random
Indians for bounty are in fact the social fist released by the
lawmakers who set up the legal and commercial offers to pay
so much per head. The army, ready to march in with bayonets
whenever the frontiersmen have brought about a superficial
situation in which *they* appear to be victims in need of rescue
and, therefore, where massacre has the local appearance of
necessary retaliation, are one other specialized feature. Back
in the settled regions, the Quakers and liberals who are horri-
fied by these events and protest vigorously, enact their part as
the social conscience, reassuring the society that it is not in
itself murderous, except for the uncontrollable few "Indian
Haters" and murderous frontiersmen. Society's conscience
as well as society's fist are independent wills that only function
socially in so far as they submit to entering as factors in
composite outcomes, most of the other factors of which are
repellent to them and involve them in what, from each side,
are unwilled outcomes.

Cooper's Hawkeye is the master invention of a powerless
figure who retains a nobility within only partially controllable
situations. His power to act is neither effective, nor does he
suspend it because it is always contaminated by the cross-

purposes of others. He is a quintessential political man with some of the resignation to messy outcomes required of any political man.

In the theoretical sections of *War and Peace*, Tolstoy discussed this same problem of the will, but was led, because his subject was war, to the choice of a passive figure, Kutuzov, as the counter-argument to the great master-player Napoleon. For Scott or Cooper the choice is not between two central figures, but between any form of action that is monarchical and has, therefore, a central, morally summarizing individual will whether it is the active will of Napoleon or the passive will of Kutuzov, and, on the other hand, forms of action that are democratic and composite with mixed and unintended results. Deerslayer is the stoic, honorable figure who, having no "actions" of his own, has nonetheless agreed to mix his will into the solutions of the actions of others. His is the stoic resignation to a contaminated outcome damaged by the violence of others. Attempting surgical, unwasteful solutions, as when in the rescue of Hist he silences but does not kill the old woman guarding her, he then becomes imbedded in the increasingly wasteful solutions of others. Captured as a result of the old woman's noisy screams, he is only freed by the massacre of the entire camp.

The plot based on a composite will, so fundamental a contribution of Scott and Cooper, reflects a society extended and morally worried, and at the same time a social life of individual and rival codes. It replicates the composite nature of competing species that Darwin describes. Its results are those of the "Hidden Hand" of Adam Smith but without the confidence that the Hidden Hand results in the good of all.

The profound analysis built into Cooper's plot is not the feeling of the inevitability of the most repulsive historical facts such as massacres. The ethical question of responsibility—who exactly is to blame and what punishment would be just?—is put aside. It is felt to be irrelevant. But such a Hegelian demonstration, because it is always the self-serving history told by the winners, remains too convenient to be acceptable. What is profound is that the deepest and most central historical facts are not so because they occur again and again directly, but because they are adjacent, secondary interferring patterns on the way to every other outcome at a given historical moment. The massacre and extermination are a secondary outcome within Cooper's plot. Along the way to recovering Hist from captivity and permitting the marriage of Chingachgook and Hist, the secondary complications and interferences of Hutter, Harry, Judith, Hetty, and Deerslayer lead to a point where the situation could only be cleared by massacre. The great, central, hard facts always occur in this way: they are incidental to thousands of other transactions that seem to have nothing to do with them and, as a secondary result to whatever primary result is intended, they again and again, as if by accident, resume the configuration of their historical solution.

In Cooper's plot we could say that on the way to the marriage of Chingachgook and Hist there was, incidentally a massacre. At a saturated moment of history every intention— such as the intention to take a journey or to marry or to farm a piece of land—will again and again register the same individual secondary outcome: and on the way to Oregon, and on the way to the marriage, and on the way to farming 240 acres in Kansas, there was a massacre, there was a massacre, there was a massacre.

7. WILDERNESS AND WILDERNESSES

The fixed geography and small set of characters in Cooper's *The Deerslayer* leads to a dancelike set of partners and positions. Once the novel begins, its entire action occurs within a closed, visible world with a set of no more than five carefully mapped out places. Each place is, in its way, like a room in a novel of manners. Whites and Indians move back and forth to

encounter each other in the camp or at the castle or the ark,
almost like the ballet of visits, dinners, and dances that makes
up a Jane Austen novel. Each scene brings together some
ever-varying smaller group of the characters who separate,
reunite, change location, invade, or flee from each of the four
primary places—Indian camp, point of land, castle, and ark.
Every one of the places is a scene of battle; most are, in the
end, the scene of violent death.

A man asleep in a canoe on a vast lake is one of the novel's
memorable notations for the small, exact location of a person
within a wilderness. The abstractness and simplicity of the
visible setting (lake, land, and the shoreline at which they
meet); the careful gradation in number, safety and property
from canoe to ark to castle to the offstage fort; the grouping
of people by pairs (Harry and Hutter, Judith and Hetty,
Leatherstocking, and Chingachgook): all point to a surveyer's
mind, at work creating the frame within which a slowly mount-
ing violent action can be displayed. Places are known by lines
of sight. As a result, descriptions have the feeling of being seen
through a surveyer's glass or the sight of a rifle.

> The fire, the canoe, and the spring near which Deerslayer
> commenced his retreat would have stood in the angles of a
> triangle of tolerably equal sides. The distance from the fire to
> the boat was a little less than the distance from the fire to the
> spring, while the distance from the spring to the boat was
> about equal to that between the two points first named. This,
> however, was in straight lines—a means of escape to which the
> fugitives could not resort. (319)

The small specks within a vast world by which orientation,
danger and safety are judged are here marked by a fire, a
canoe, a spring. For every place where someone stands there
is an exact goal (the canoe in this case) and an enemy that is
just about to get there first. In Chapter 20, to take only one
example, Judith and Hetty, in one canoe, race back to safety

in the ark, but pursued by three Hurons in a second canoe, traveling in the women's wake, and steadily overtaking them. The map is exact in the mind. Again there are three points and a mathematical problem. Will the first canoe, slower but nearer the ark, reach safety before the second, faster canoe covers the longer distance and cuts them off?

> As yet, the Indians had not been able to get nearer to the girls than two hundred yards, though they were what seamen would term "in their wake," or in a direct line behind them, passing over the same track of water. This made the pursuit what is technically called a "stern chase," which is proverbially a "long chase," the meaning of which is that in consequence of the relative positions of the parties, no change becomes apparent except that which is a direct gain in the nearest possible approach. (390-1)

Cooper's reader always has in his hand a map of this kind, and within the novel the larger, less graspable landscape becomes familiar in the end because patch after patch of it has been crisscrossed with precisely mapped moments of danger. The reader is made the explorer, not the settler of this landscape. Like the map of a battlefield, there is no "trace" of events other than their narrative. Events like the canoe race, the negotiations, the rescue of Hurry Harry, all of which take place on the water, are perfect images of a history without traces. Under the lake itself, the unmarkable graves of the Hutter family slowly increase in number: the wife has been buried there for years, Hutter himself is lowered under the surface in the middle of the novel, Hetty joins them at the end. Hutter's wealth from water (as a pirate), his settlement on water (the ark and castle), his grave under water, make him the symbol of a futile and erasable civilization.

The exact, small-scale geography of Cooper's world is a product of its lines of sight, its points of measurement and quantification, its few reference points, and its procedure of giving reality to paths and spaces by walking, racing, creeping silently, or paddling a canoe along and through them towards a visible goal. These features occur under the alert spell of danger, a constant danger whose purpose is not so much excitement, as it is the demand for absolute sensory attention. Look down this path as if your life depended on it; judge how far it is to the ark and how fast the second canoe is closing in on you as if your life depended on it; judge how distracted the Indians at the fire are by the ivory elephant as if your life depended on it.

But the larger "world" of *The Deerslayer* is not simply a sum of patches mapped out under momentary conditions of endangered attentiveness. Nor is it a series of paintings in the formal landscape styles of Claude Lorrain and Salvator Rosa. Such set pieces, posed groupings frozen for description, are bravura imitations in a period of illustrated novels, but of less importance than the rational maps of action.[23] The wilderness is not approximated by either of these miniaturizing devices and Cooper's solution to its representation was one of his most important contributions to the novel, particularly the European novel.

For the novel, Cooper invented not the setting but the environment. Nature understood as environment is no longer seen as setting, as the aesthetically experienced location of persons and acts. Setting is literally the background against which or in front of which human, psychological events occur as a foreground. Environment on the other hand is the play of forces that gives life a specific shape. From Montesquieu's *L'Esprit des Lois* to Darwin's *Origin of Species* the exact study of life forms under differing environmental conditions developed so that the variations of culture, temperament, laws, psychologies, appropriate skills, and survival tactics had been differentiated by climate, by the set of competitors, by struggles for the basic goods of life. It is within an environment, in this technical sense of the word, that each of Cooper's

Leatherstocking Tales takes place. Cooper moves the novel outdoors, taking it out of society and into an environment. Here the laws of territory and relative force, the ultimate simple questions of survival and reproduction, the matching of appropriate skills and capacities for endurance to the details of the forces, both of the physical environment and of the competing animal and human groups, the hierarchy of predators and the simple binary outcome of extinction or survival, become the basic elements.

The redescription of the world as a spectrum of environments is one of the great accomplishments of 19th-century science. Economics, anthropology, and Darwinian natural history all contributed to a revolution that overthrew the universal nature of the Enlightenment, the nature of "scenes" and "pictures," and replaced it with the selective operation of forces, the varied outcomes (temporary and diverse) of struggle. Only when nature assumes its 19th-century meaning is it appropriate to speak of the wilderness in Cooper as "nature." As an environment the world is not marked by sudden eruptions of cataclysmic natural forces—storms, volcanoes, ice, landslides—for these are the 18th century's irrational, randomizing projections of a nature that acts at cross-purposes with the daily, incremental work of reason. The earthquakes described by Kleist and Voltaire are the best examples of the 18th-century mind's account of the "irrationality" of natural forces. Instead, for Cooper or Darwin, for the 19th-century account of environment, steady, continuous pressures to which all groups adapt and accommodate themselves over time, but some more successfully than others, are the key feature of the natural world. Those forces that elicit skill, those conditions of life that differentiate and give advantage to a certain build, a certain temperament, a certain preferred food source or habit of grouping: these are the features that make nature and environment. The single most frequently stressed word in *The Deerslayer* is the word "gifts" and under this word is hidden a

Darwinian account of style and skills, temperamental and social traits, that when summed up point towards extinction or dominance.

That Cooper resettled the novel outdoors, made of it a form of physical action, rather than conversation and inner sensibility, repopulated it with male rather than female characters, centered its subject on death rather than marriage, or, on survival by means of avoiding death rather than on generational survival by means of marriage and children—these features are intimately related to his making his world an environment of forces in which the central fact of struggle takes place. For struggle, the remote form is the contest, but the central act is the fight to the death between opponents only one of whom can survive, both on the individual level and on that of the group. This struggle is the structuring principle of the historical novel as a form.

Leatherstocking's battle to the death over the canoes, Hurry Harry's wrestling match with the Indians over the castle, and the final assembly of all the Indians and all the whites on the point of land from which only one group will walk away: these are the external events of the world seen as an environment. Within the environment, opponents are tested and matched again and again. Speed, courage, cunning, aim with a rifle, stealth, cooperative effort, strength, resourcefulness: a sequence of contests resettles the hierarchy of persons and groups.

The most significant use of Cooper's skeletal framework, his environmental novel, was not for later descriptions of the wilderness itself, not for the exploration of nature. Rather it was the novel of the city, the quintessential 19th-century environment, that saw Cooper's invention in its true light. It is the ease with which the emotional and structural details of Cooper's wilderness environment could be transposed for the representation of the urban world that made him the first American writer (and, in the end, the only American writer of the 19th century) to enter the new "world literature" of which

Goethe was the first to speak. Cooper, like Kafka in the 20th century, invented an immediately comprehensible solution for the description of an unprecedented reality. In the English or French traditions of the novel, the features of the urban environment were accommodated by means of an enlarged form of the small-town novel of manners; or alternately, as in Dickens, or later in James, by using the collapse of the form to give a negative rendering. Cooper's adventure form, along with the detective form (itself a variant of the novel of manners), solved and made representable the urban reality by seeing it as a play of forces, a new wilderness whose key actors were solitary figures rather than families or small-scale, knowable communities. With this accomplishment Cooper, whatever his place in the parochial 19th-century American novel, made the first American contribution to world literature. Balzac's great enthusiasm for Cooper is the most important point of transfer, but Baudelaire, Hugo, Dostoevsky, and Zola all represent in their works the states of endangered, solitary motion through a wilderness of forces that Cooper made the key emotional state of his novels. The city with its unexpected events, its dangers and sudden encounters with strangers, its direct and total challenge to the single, isolated figure, is as outside the structured social world of the small-town novel as the wilderness is. Like Cooper's forest the city is also a world of night, of intensified forces and dangers, and the city, like all environments, creates a preoccupation with personal styles that condenses skills and temperament into a smooth, unified state of preparedness for whatever experience or test might occur next. Leatherstocking and the poetic dandy of Baudelaire, the Hemingway hero and Rastignac or Raskolnikov are all figures of alert, unified style that anticipates the contests of an environment of forces to which they alone, without delegates or assistants, will have to answer.

Darwin's journal of the voyage of the Beagle appeared in 1839, one year before *The Deerslayer*. In hindsight we can date a fundamental change in the central meaning of the word

Nature from Darwin's book and the theoretical analysis that followed. Cooper's novel imbedded the American experience, and, in particular, the white beginnings in America within categories of struggle, the competition to survive, the relative value of traits (here called "gifts") under the tests of life and death competition. The hard facts of this picture without the trappings of religious mission or democratic philosophy, without the noble background of flight from persecution or the noble future of individual opportunity or nation building, and entirely without compacts and self-government, are the hard facts of *The Deerslayer*: one place, two men, two guns, one survivor.

Both *Walden* and *Moby Dick* would seem, at first sight, to be works of the same American moment. Both appear to base human action and meanings within an environment. For *Walden*, the experimental side of Thoreau's adventure was the empirical question of what the laws, moods, spiritual order, and symbolic possibilities of the particular small world of land and water were and, at the same time, what the fundamental acts of daily human life were. The force of the seasons, the kind of shelter needed within this climate, the simplest nourishing crops that might be grown here would all be given for this environment. But deeper background questions were also environmentally given. Would it be possible for one person alone to survive here? Did an unarmed man stand a chance against the animals? Were there rival claimants for the space? That each of these questions does not even have to be addressed shows the suburban nature of the environment that Thoreau has chosen: a mild climate without predators, unclaimed and without hostile societies. These are the features of a life lived, if not in a peaceful society, at least nearby one so that the cover of its previous acts of clearing and of its present power of self-protection extend out over the experiment even without his having to acknowledge it.

Moby Dick is much more accurately a world of forces and food, a particular set of laws of the climate of the sea, a configuration of personal and moral styles of human behavior and thought that have developed in response to that array of conditions, a philosophy and heroic standard unique to the conditions of this specific world with its inner logic. In other words, the determined, selective laws of survival and specialization are at work and in the hands of the sea. It is essential in environments that the forces of the particular world dwarf the human will: as the forest does in Cooper, the sea in Melville, the city in Baudelaire or Dickens, the land in Hardy. Melville's sea is the environment of a human world, but one so vast that no property is ever claimed. Sailors are even more spread out over the surface of the sea than the hunting groups of Indians were over the surface of America, or the Eskimos over the Arctic. Melville's environment, while it selects (there are no women, children, or old) and creates the styles that face it (Stubb's as well as Ahab's), is, nonetheless, not the world as Malthus or Darwin defined it: a world crowded with rival claimants for the same niche of life, a world with too many for all to survive.

Insofar as *Walden* or *Moby Dick* are fundamental myths of America, they erect conditions that are more peaceful than those of Cooper's *The Deerslayer*. *Walden* is exceptional in that the experiment can be run within what appears to be the environment, but is in fact the already pacified and cleared annex of a society: its backyard or park. While retaining an unconquerable world, *Moby Dick* chooses to emphasize the forces of will and the giving of meaning by choosing the one world so vast that there is no competitor and so simplified that above its surface only man can move at all.

No one went beyond Cooper's solemn and wondrous account of the wilderness until Jack London sixty years later. Cooper's forest is a summer world, an almost empty world of highly differentiated beautiful places with views and paths. Although still unsettled, these aesthetically powerful locations are like the as yet unclaimed ideal sites for future homes. There is a forward-looking side to the natural world that

Cooper describes: the vistas and prospects are there, the near and far "points of interest," but not yet the porches or windows that will frame the view correctly and make it the aesthetic property of some home owner who will share it with his guests. The world is seen through the windows of a series of as yet unbuilt houses.

At the same time the very building of these houses will destroy the solemnity and power of the wilderness by putting it into a human scale and clearing it. What is meant by the wilderness in Cooper is something temporary and fragile seen through the eyes of its future destroyer. That Leatherstocking is a hunter makes it conspicuous that he is the first installment of irresistible power. He never misses. Francis Parkman's concise statement of the goal of his first great history, *The Conspiracy of Pontiac*, describes Cooper's novel as well: "It aims to portray the American forest and the American Indian at the period when both received their final doom."[24]

Jack London, half a century later, had absorbed the Darwinian picture and had broadened the scene of the wilderness from land not yet conquered and settled, to land unconquerable and permanently hostile to settlement. What was meant by "nature" in the time of Wordsworth or Cooper was true of only a small fraction of the surface of the earth. When oceans, deserts, arctic, and tropics are added in to what we mean by wilderness, the earth comes to seem inhospitable and defiant. In this enlarged world the relation of man to nature focuses on the single and permanently open questions of survival, and not on the question of how rapid or drawn-out human conquest and destruction will be. The sea, the desert, the arctic, the tropics (altogether 90 percent of the surface of the earth) can hardly be marked by man, let alone destroyed. For London it is man that is fragile against forces that make a rifle a puny symbol. These are the forces of time and individual aging as well as those of space, temperature, and scarcity.

In the 1840s the wilderness of Cooper, Thoreau, and Parkman was best imagined as a lake or pond, a grove of trees, a

herd of buffalo, a camp of Indians. The rapacious hands of
the white settlers were already at the throat of each. The
sound of a new, highly efficient American ax in the forest was
a symbolic first touch of that power. A rifle shot and a fallen
buffalo meant that as soon as they wanted, the whites could
erase the herds. The boat on the pond, the Indian dead by the
canoe, and the train that Thoreau saw coming along the edge
of Walden Pond were the first installments of irresistible
power. The forest from which Cooper, Parkman, and Thoreau
think out the image of nature, although they call it "woods" is
already nearly a "park." The national parks are controlled
settings for the experience of wilderness. It is unimaginable
that we will ever have to set aside part of the Pacific Ocean to
provide the "experience" of the ocean or part of the Antarctic
for the "experience" of polar ice.

The very idea of stopping to "have an experience," the
central subject of middle-class psychology and ethics from
Wordsworth to Thoreau to Proust to Virginia Woolf, to
Frost and T.S. Eliot; the idea of life as a series of moments, a
set of experiences of "really" seeing or "really" feeling intensely
alive—this idea is the product of a highly charged self-consciousness, even self-absorption, in a setting of fragile and
vanishing conditions, but without the absorbing and prior
problem of surviving and providing. For Proust or Woolf
these vanishing conditions are those of an aristocracy, a genteel
world. Once again, the analogy within American experience
was to the about-to-vanish noble forests, Indians, and buffalo
which were the Guermantes and Swanns and Mrs. Ramseys
of American life.

By the time of Jack London and Hemingway a more in-
exhaustible opponent had taken over from Cooper's soon to
be surveyed and cleared forest. Since the central action within
the wilderness had always been warfare, Cooper's forward-
looking fears are really an anticipation of peace and victory.
With peace and the defeat of the various groups that claim the
land, the more fundamental destruction of the civilizing process

would begin. Just as the forest is temporary and fragile, so too
is the state of war that Cooper describes. By the time of
London and Hemingway, the wilderness, once again the setting of warfare, has been altered by two revolutions in the
nature of war: one Darwinian and the other a result of the
murderous, mass slaughter introduced in the American Civil
War. Darwinian warfare is permanent, not the prelude to a
peace brought about by conquest, and it is this Darwinian
battle between the species that is London's revision of Cooper.
The Darwinian struggle implies, as well, a tacit war between
the old and useless and the young. The old are unable to
provide, and live at the expense of the young on whom they
are, in times of plenty, an annoyance, and in times of scarcity,
a burden that must be sacrificed for the survival of providers.
London's story, "The Law of Life," is the best account of this
Darwinian warfare and its transformation of the meaning of
wilderness. In Cooper the warfare is between different societies, different stages of civilization. The novels are written by
and for those who were the winners and who can, therefore,
pay the tribute of regret and admiration to their worthy
victims. The wars between wolves and men, dogs and wolves,
man and cold, man and sea, are wars of the Darwinian kind,
and they impose a new meaning on the wilderness in which
they occur.

The second revision of warfare is more central in Hemingway, Cooper's greatest descendent. Hemingway's *For Whom
the Bell Tolls* updates the Leatherstocking Tales by setting its
hero in a camp, among figures slightly alien in culture, a small
group of men and women in a confusing war, set in a natural
world of mountains, caves, trees, and paths, with cycles of
love and killing, tests of style and craft, but now within
warfare for which the best novels always come from the losing
side (like *All Quiet on the Western Front*) or in which even
the winners write novels of small-scale action in which they
were defeated (as in *The Red Badge of Courage*, or *A Farewell
to Arms* or *The Naked and the Dead*). The death of the

central figure, with which such novels often end, the futility of war, the confusion and pointlessness of the small-scale events described are all details of the revision of warfare itself brought about by the machine gun, the trench, the drawn-out slaughters of the American Civil War and World War I. The natural world of rain and mud is the inevitable image for the slow wearing away of morale, the confusion and inability to move, let alone conquer, that is the standard narrative description of the new mass warfare of conscripted armies.

As the solider is worn down, discarded, replaced by fresh recruits, the static inexorable pressure of the battlefield, the war itself, the mud and rain goes on. It is the experience of the common soldier towards which the modern account is aimed. The warfare in Cooper is, by contrast, a world of clean shots, a world of "aim." The perfect aim of Hawkeye and of any sharpshooter becomes indifferent, although when he is about to die on the final page of *For Whom the Bell Tolls*, Robert Jordan sets himself up, proud of his aim, determined to take as many as he can along with him to death.

The emphasis on aim and, with it, personal control, the choice of the moment to fire, the selection of a victim, all point towards a rational and meaningful account of warfare. Where everything depends on the soldier's aim, the war itself is likely to have clearly defined aims and a code of correct and proscribed acts. The natural world that encloses this warfare is itself ordered and noble. The tall, ancient trees of Cooper's forest are its best signs. The warfare is primarily the sum of a set of heroic individuals, the moments of combat are as much contests between heroes as those in Homer's *Iliad*. The outcomes are proportional to honor and skill. Both Leatherstocking and Rivenoak survive in *The Deerslayer*.

Cooper's larger purpose in his novel gives a separate, less conscious, meaning to the word "aim." The precision of Deerslayer is made composite with the clumsiness and moral coarseness of all those by his side. In the final act his perfect aim is not good enough, once he is outnumbered and sur-

rounded. The massacre that overrides his rational violence
requires little aiming, only superior numbers and a certain
amount of time. Similarly the surgical aim of Cooper's plot,
its finite purpose (the rescue of Hist and the marriage that will
follow) is subject to a similar historical override and the
composite outcome of massacre and extermination are brought
about without it being acknowledged that they were themselves the social aim.

By the end of Cooper's novel, Leatherstocking, newly freed
from captivity, stands for the essential American freedom. No
longer surrounded or tied down, his freedom has been won.
Such freedom is not innate or automatic. It is a recovered
freedom in the sense Yeats used in describing how the soul
"recovers radical innocence."[25] Radical freedom has the inner
burden that it has been recovered by "regrettable" means. The
land at the end of Cooper's novel has been reclaimed by nature,
but now its surface is strewn with bones. The land and freedom
are both pictured by Cooper as ready for life, their pre-history
has ended. The stages of that life are marked by beginnings
stained with violence. As biography *The Deerslayer* gives
Leatherstocking two features that allow him to begin his life:
first, he has taken an adult name and left youth behind. The
cost is one dead Indian. Second, he has been endowed with
recovered freedom, radical freedom (at the cost of a massacre).
Now his history begins.

2

Making a Thing into a Man:
The Sentimental Novel and Slavery

In the same year that Cooper's *The Deerslayer* appeared, Catherine Beecher's *A Treatise on Domestic Economy* was published. This 1841 edition was revised in collaboration with her sister Harriet Beecher Stowe and published as *The American Woman's Home* in 1869. The years 1841 and 1869 bracket the Civil War, which broke out officially in 1861, and they bracket, as well, the publication of *Uncle Tom's Cabin* in 1851 by Harriet Beecher Stowe. In her household manual Catherine Beecher proposed nothing less than a rational, simplified, and democratic household. Such a home would provide an intensified definition of the family as those who share the work of a house without the need of permanent help. At the same time, the simplifications and ingenious inventions which Beecher described suggested one solution to the "soft slavery" of a class of domestic servants whose existence was clearly incompatible with democratic life. The beginning of the emancipation of the housewife from an onerous life of toil, along with the goal of eliminating household servants, link the more commonplace restructuring of the home proposed by Beecher to the larger restructuring of the national home that is the subject of *Uncle Tom's Cabin*.

The importance of the organization of the kitchen work space and the simplification of actions in the interest of efficiency make Beecher's book of profound interest to the

architectural historian Sigfried Giedion who, in his classic
history, *Mechanization Takes Command*, makes of her work
an analytic breakthrough for the home on the order of the
later Taylor System of time and motion studies for the factory.
Between the 1840s and the 1950s, the ongoing series of inventions and simplifications that eliminated the drudgery of house-
work, and along with that drudgery, the necessity of servants,
made possible the inner emancipation for women expressed in
the *Treatise on Domestic Economy*. Only a family small in
scale and with its tasks reduced to those capable of completion
by the cooperative work of the family members themselves
could fulfill the image of a democratic household life.

Beecher's book shares many goals with Thoreau's *Walden*,
which appeared in 1854, some thirteen years later. In *Walden*
the possibility of independence and full selfhood are linked to
the discovery and description of a simple and rational house
and a round of tasks that permit self-sufficiency and even
poetry. Thoreau's tidy and minimal hearth, home, garden,
and pond were not however, designed for family life. Therefore, it could not miniaturize the ideal relations of the nation
itself, since the center of any political representation must
include continuity, and therefore reproduction. Nonetheless,
the spirit of work and domesticity as pleasureable and not
necessarily tied to degrading toil, the exhilaration of the everyday round of life, and, finally, the political significance of the
smallest repeatable unit—the self-sufficient household—joins
Thoreau's philosophical experiment to Beecher's more commonplace utopia of pots and pans.

The ultimate topic of Beecher's *Treatise*, of her sister's
novel, *Uncle Tom's Cabin*, and of Thoreau's *Walden* is the
topic of freedom seen from the angle of intimate servitude.
The interior of a house is the point of departure for each
writer. The politics of domestic order reflects a national order,
and its transformation or improvement makes possible an
imaginative refounding of democracy. At the same time,
Beecher, Stowe, and Thoreau provide the indoor images for

the Jeffersonian Yeoman farm, usually described only in its masculine, outdoor images of field and plow, harvest and planting. Ever since the appearance of Henry Nash Smith's *Virgin Land* and Leo Marx's *The Machine in the Garden*, the privileged setting of that Jeffersonian pastoral America of small farms, family life, independent and steady work has been seen as a central myth of 19th-century American life.[1] Both Smith and Marx explore only the masculine, outdoors half of the Jeffersonian farm. They conflate what I would like to separate as two distinct privileged settings—the wilderness and the farm. Or rather, as Leo Marx points out, they explore the contradictions built into a set of American images that require features from two incompatible stages of civilization, the wilderness and the garden that by degrees replaces it.

To show the extent to which it is only the masculine side of the Yeoman farm that is in view it is only necessary to quote one famous description from Crevècoeur's *Letters From An American Farmer* of 1782.

> Some few towns excepted, we are all tillers of the earth, from Nova Scotia to West Florida. We are a people of cultivators, scattered over an immense territory, communicating with each other by means of good roads and navigable rivers, united by the silken bands of mild government, all respecting the laws, without dreading their power, because they are equitable. We are all animated by the spirit of an industry that is unfettered and unrestrained, because each person works for himself. If he travels through our rural districts he views not the hostile castle, and the haughty mansion, contrasted with the clay-built hut and miserable cabin, where cattle and men help to keep each other warm, and dwell in meanness, smoke and indigence. A pleasing uniformity of decent competence appears throughout our habitations. The meanest of our log-houses is a dry and comfortable habitation.[2]

The "tillers of the soil," each of whom "works for himself" and lives in "a pleasing uniformity of decent competence" in what can only be called a domesticity of comfort and hard work, are evoked here as a masculine race of builders and farmers. The complementary images to this outdoors world, in which even the homes are seen by a traveler who does not enter them, were provided by Harriet Beecher Stowe in *Uncle Tom's Cabin.*

> A quiet scene now rises before us. A large, roomy, neatly painted kitchen, its yellow floor glossy and smooth, and without a particle of dust; a neat well-blacked cooking stove; rows of shining tin, suggestive of unmentionable good things to the appetite; glossy, green wood chairs, old and firm; a small flag-bottomed rocking chair, with a patchwork cushion in it, neatly contrived out of small pieces of different colored woolen goods, a larger sized one, motherly and old, whose wide arms breathed hospitable invitation, seconded by the solicitation of its feather cushions—a real comfortable persuasive old chair, and worth, in the way of honest, homely enjoyment, a dozen of your plush or brochetelle drawing-room gentry; and in the chair, gently swaying back and forward, her eyes bent on some fine sewing, sat our old friend Eliza.[3]

Stowe, like Crevecoeur, solemnizes the common world. Hers is female and indoors, his male and outdoors. Crevecoeur's passage ends with the ringing words, "We have no princes, for whom we toil, starve and bleed: we are the most perfect society now existing in the world."[4] Stowe's world of comfort and diligence comes to focus on an old rocking chair in which we find "our old friend Eliza," a runaway slave. The capacity of the sentimental novel not only to build in, but to build itself around, the hard fact of slavery underlines the advantage of the female, indoor picture and its available form, sentimentality, over the masculine side of the same myth traced by Henry Nash Smith and Leo Marx. The masculine, outdoor world had as its available form the adventure novel, a form that has as its central tension the divided loyalties of the male, his revolt against domestic life and his need for it. The superficial rejection of social and domestic life as a style, takes place in novels whose plots have no other goal than the rescue or reestablishment of that domestic life—a farm safe from marauding Indians, a town free of gunmen. The masculine novel has its eye fixed on what might be called a secondary problem of the Jeffersonian pastoral world of peaceful, hard-working farmers. That secondary problem is the reluctance in the male to reject the heroic side of his energies, which had been needed when settlements were first made, but were now irrelevant and even dangerous once those settlements had entered their mature, unheroic Jeffersonian form. The male conflict between archaic, but heroic, childhood and the uninteresting and subordinate toil of the pastoral ideal once it is completely in place, blinds the adventure novel to what was the deeper problem in the American setting. As a result, the central fable of slavery in America was written by a woman. Its setting was the indoors half of the Jeffersonian household and not primarily the fields beyond, and it found to hand the most radical popular form available to middle-class culture, the sentimental novel.

1. Sentimentality and Irony

It has usually been taken as one more reason to sneer at the cranky old man that Tolstoy had become by the time that he wrote *What Is Art* that he named *Uncle Tom's Cabin* as one of the few genuine modern works of art.[5] While calling attention to the humanitarian greatness of Stowe's novel, Tolstoy was engaged in an angry and morally indignant denunciation of the ironic and decadent literature which he chiefly identified with the novels and poetry of later 19th-century French culture, a literature that had become and would remain throughout the literary period of modernism the aesthetic norm for western literature. The tradition of thought and feeling out of which Tolstoy was writing is now so little understood in either its aesthetics or its politics that the only remaining use for such words as sentimentalism or sentimentality is to point out flaws of representation, signs of weakness or evasiveness about moral or emotional reality, and false consciousness of a particularly contemptuous kind. All that is cheap, self-flattering, idealizing, and deliberately dishonest we think of as sentimentality. Self-indulgent, rhetorical, coy: at times sentimentality seems to include all of the moral flaws that the honesty, sobriety and objectivity of literary realism were designed to correct.

Yet in its earliest stages the development of psychological realism and sentimentality were closely connected, as they are, for example, in the works of Richardson, Sterne, and Rousseau.[6] Of even greater importance is the fact that from roughly 1740 to 1860 sentimentality was a crucial tactic of politically radical representation throughout western culture. Until it was replaced by the strategies of literary naturalism, class struggle, anger, and counterforce in the last third of the 19th century, the liberal humanism of sentimentality was the primary radical methodology within culture.[7] There is an intimate connection between sentimentality and the rise of the novel as a central and popular cultural form. Because sentimentality depends upon an inward and empathic emotional bond, it connects, in its intimate presentation of ordinary life, in particularly rich ways to the possibilities of the novel: a private, domestic, intimate form. Sentimentality is a fundamental moral evidence of the dominance of the middle class in literature just as epic objectivity is the moral trace of aristocratic dominance. I believe that it can accurately be said that the entire history of the novel as a popular form is critically tied to its sentimental texture and to its melodramatic scheme of action. The two are nearly inseparable. The campaign to purge the novel, generally by means of irony, of its sentimental texture, a campaign that accelerates after Flaubert and James, spells the end of the novel as a popular form, or rather divides the novel into, on the one hand, a popular form of entertainment, and, on the other, a high art form in which the elimination of sentimentality is a central goal.

Within the history of the novel an even stronger statement can be made. The presence of sentimentality is most obvious at precisely those places where an essential extension of the subject matter of the novel itself is taking place. Just where new materials, new components of the self, new types of heroes and heroines, new subjects of mood and feeling occur: at exactly those places will the presence of sentimentality be most marked.

The entire sentimental procedure is already present in the novels of Richardson in the 1740s: The extended central scenes of dying and deathbeds, mourning and loss, the rhetorical treatment of the central theme of suffering, the creation of the prisoner as the central character, the themes of imprisonment, the violation of selfhood, power relations in the intimate and familiar territory, freedom, the centrality of the family and the definition of the power of literary representation in terms of tears—the novel as a "tear jerker" or as a "three-handkerchief" novel. From Richardson and Sterne to Rousseau to Wordsworth to Irving and Stowe, Dickens and Hugo, Dostoevsky and Tolstoy himself, sentimentality often marks precisely the point within accepted patterns of feeling and representation where radical revision is taking place. With Richardson and Sterne the point is obvious, but Rousseau's dramatic expansion in *la nouvelle Héloïse* of the theme of love, Scott's introduction of history into the novel, Hugo's and Dicken's introduction of the urban world, Dostoevsky's, no less than Sterne's psychology of the irrational— each of these highly experimental matters, along with the use of children, slaves, and the old as central characters, first occurs within the novel accompanied by a prominent sentimental texture and a melodramatic scheme of action. In later American Culture the works of Twain, Frost, Hemingway, and many others preserved the core of sentimental technique even in the process of adapting it to later conditions or obscuring it beneath a veneer of toughness, elegance, or self-irony. With the early films of Charlie Chaplin the entire repertoire of sentimental assumptions and procedures returns at a critical cultural moment, the transfer of major cultural priority from the novel to the film.

In her study *The Popular Novel in England*, J. M. S. Tompkins writes of the concept of Sensibility, using the term in a way that cannot be easily differentiated from what I am calling Sentimentality.

> Sensibility was a modern quality; it was not found among the ancients, but was a product of modern conditions; the heroic and tremendous virtues might be dying out with the stormy times that evoked them, but modern security, leisure and education had evolved a delicacy of sensation, a refinement of virtue, which the age found more beautiful. The human sympathies which a rougher age had repressed, expanded widely, especially towards the weak and unfortunate, and the social conscience began to occupy itself with prisoners, children, animals and slaves.[8]

Tomkin's list is a revealing one. In fact, each of her categories could be described as prisoners: children of their parents, animals of their owners, prisoners of the state, slaves of their masters. Each was subject to abuse and tyranny. Each was, by moral and legal custom, deprived of that degree of selfhood that is dependent upon rights and freedom, autonomy, and the primacy of self-interest.

It was, of course, Rousseau who described all men within society as prisoners when at the beginning of *The Social Contract* he wrote, "Man is born free, and everywhere he is in chains." Wordworth described the relation of adulthood to the full humanity of childhood as a growing up in which "shades of the prison house begin to fall."

From the general imprisonment of all men in society the sentimental analogy argues to the need for freedom and full humanity in individual cases. In each of Tompkins's four categories—prisoners, children, animals, and slaves—the weak and the helpless within society gain by means of sentimental experience full representation through the central moral category of compassion. The theory of compassion, its relation to the politically active side of the sentimental novel, I will develop at a later point. For now it is enough to note that the revision of status, once accomplished, leaves behind it the ongoing sentimental images that, once we have forgotten the prior cruelty and denial of selfhood, linger on as the kind of image-making that we now associate with the Disney films of animal life or the Victorian album literature of childhood. To mistake the after-effects of politically successful sentimental representation for the representation itself is a particularly obtuse 20th-century mistake.

Because the struggle against sentimentality is so closely identified with the modern period I would like briefly to contrast an example of the modern historical strategy with *Uncle Tom's Cabin* as a way to prepare for a deeper account of sentimental representation. A little more than a hundred years after Stowe's novel, a major novel appeared during the civil rights movement, just as Stowe's novel had within the abolitionist movement. This later novel created, like Stowe's, a scandal and a debate at the meeting point of current political action, history, and the ideological premises of representation. Styron's *Nat Turner* embodies precisely what I take to be the representational strategy of the modern period as Stowe's sentimental strategy was for her own period.

Styron's novel is first of all psychological and interior, a variant of the dramatic monologue. It involves what I would like to call a Romance of Consciousness: an exotic, morally adventurous identification on the part of the reader with the inner world of an outlaw, and an outlaw at the life-moment of maximum intensity. The frame of the novel involves the telling of his life by Turner himself in the brief period between his capture and his execution, between his uprising and slaughter of the whites and his own death.

Nat Turner as a central figure for an investigation of slavery involves the modern choice of the exceptional over the typical for the analysis of social experience. Not only is Turner unique in his revolt, he is from childhood on unique in being the only slave in Virginia taught to read, the only slave to own a book, and so on. As an inventive master carpenter and as a preacher he is even an artist of sorts and it is as disguised artists that all modern outsiders—madmen, criminals, blacks and Jews—appear.

Stowe's novel, on the other hand, is objective and systematic. Its topic is not the mind of the slave but the system of slavery itself in its normal and diverse operations. Like the novels of Zola, *Uncle Tom's Cabin* links its form to the economics of a sector of work with its typical figures, inevitable experiences, its primary settings and the interconnections with the basic experiences and ages of life. Thus Uncle Tom moves through three economic varieties of slavery, each of which represents the forms and severities, the benefits and experiences of slavery within one of the three classes of southern society. From the middle-class farming world of Kentucky to the upper-class urban household of New Orleans to the lower-class plantation of Simon Legree, the life elements are determined by climate, economics, and scale of need in a conspicuous way. The variety of slaves and experiences are similarly objective and systematic. Psychology is relegated to a marginal position.

As we turn from method to action we find a similar contrast between the two novels. The structure of action within Styron's novel is not melodrama but irony, dramatic and historical irony. We begin and end the novel with the slaughter, and the reader therefore experiences every detail of Turner's early life as a clue to the future slaughter. Every moment of his suffering is only partly suffering because the reader is aware of the coming revenge and nothing so eliminates the reality of suffering as the structure of revenge or the anticipation of revenge. Every insult is only partly an insult because the bloody sword hangs over the scene, visible to the reader but not yet to any of the historical actors.

It is the ironic power of fated violence that is the essential modernist structuring device. *Nat Turner* belongs to that familiar contemporary crime genre of which Mailer's *The Executioner's Song*, Capote's *In Cold Blood*, and such best sellers as Rosser's *Looking For Mr. Goodbar* are familiar examples. In this genre ordinary life is viewed within the frame of irrational, absurd violence. The details of life are experienced by the reader under the sign of an as-yet-post-poned bloody destruction. In such books the entire lingering over the catalog of ordinary experience occurs primarily to give existential weight and an air of reasonableness to a single act of insane violence which the reader, who has been placed in the position of the murderer rather than that of the victim, is encouraged to find, at least for the moment, reasonable and satisfying. Historical irony is the possession by the reader of the single apocalyptic fact unknown to the actors that, if known to them, would render meaningless or desperate every single everyday gesture. Historical irony of the modern kind (the viewpoint of the hidden observer who cannot warn the victims he watches and observes as only the murderer also observes) is in fact, the most unhistorical strategy possible. No point of view so corrodes the actual meaning of the past as lived experience as the one that sees it as the doomed and unconscious prelude to an irrational catastrophe of which the future alone is in possession of the knowledge.

The scheme of action within Stowe's novel depends upon an inevitable and fated suffering, not upon a violent and sudden action. As I will try to show later, the time scheme of action within the sentimental novel is one of its key features. At the same time, the record of suffering and death, both for Tom and for Little Eva, is balanced by the equally melo-dramatic deliverance and escape of George and Eliza.

The three main elements of the strategy— (1) the irony of

unexpected and apocalyptic violence as the strategy of action; (2) the interior monologue of a unique central figure intensified to the point of derangement, a central figure who is the killer and not the victim; (3) the goal of giving existential weight and reasonableness to single climactic acts—all three derive from a tradition that begins with Dostoevsky's *Crime and Punishment*, a novel that even while retaining key elements of sentimental technique, reversed it with the technique that I have called the Romance of Consciousness.

Like the classic American romance, the modern form depends upon a suspension of ordinary conditions in order to identify, for a time, with exceptional states. As in the traditional romance, this fictive identification ends with a return, on the reader's part, to the normal world. His or her need for the exotic and the intense was both set in play and satisfied in order to prevent its activation in real life. A writer like Norman Mailer plays out this conservative function of the Romance of Consciousness as the very role of the writer himself. Whites, Negroes, boxers, murderers: the historical role-playing it totally safe precisely because of its extremity. It is, in the words of Nelson Algren's title, *A Walk on the Wild Side*.

Like the Romance of Consciousness which I have identified as the modern historical form, the Sentimental Novel depends upon experimental, even dangerous, extensions of the self of the reader. It is, therefore, not realistic. Unlike the modern form it draws on novel *objects* of feeling rather than novel feelings. As its center is the experimental extension of normality, that is, of normal states of primary feeling to people from whom they have been previously withheld. It involves the experimental lending out of normality rather than the experimental borrowing of abnormality as in the modern form. This experimental loaning out of normality assumes that normality—full human normality—is itself a prized possession and not yet an object of boredom and contempt, as normality is in the modern Romance of Consciousness. Sentimentality is, therefore, a romance of the object rather than a romance of the subject. It is anti-ironic in exactly the degree that the modern ironic form is anti-sentimental.

2. Politics of Normality

The political content of sentimentality is democratic in that it experiments with the extension of full and complete humanity to classes of figures from whom it has been socially withheld. The typical objects of sentimental compassion are the prisoner, the madman, the child, the very old, the animal, and the slave. Each achieves, or rather earns, the right to human regard by means of the reality of their suffering. It has to be remembered that in the 18th century it was common to visit asylums to be entertained by the antics of the mad. The withholding of humanity is an active and not merely a negligent fact. In literature such withholding is indicated by either absence or by comedy. In Stowe's novel, she indicates in the comic pair Sam and Andy the comic roles that in earlier literature were the sign of this withholding. Of course, the absence of blacks in literature in which central human experiences were recorded is the counterpart to this comic presence.

The objects of sentimentality were historically subject to both cruelty and neglect. Recent social historians of the family, such as Stone, have documented this thoroughly in the case of children. Certainly, the greatest achievement of sentimentality was the part that it played in creating full human reality for children.[9] It is one of the sophisticated elements of Stowe's sentimental strategy in *Uncle Tom's Cabin* that she has both a slave and a child at the center of her novel, or rather that she interposes between the reader and the slave, a child. By doing this she is able to borrow from the nearly completed historical sentimentalization of the child, the energy to begin the more difficult and historically risky sentimentalization of the black slave.

All that now seems excessive and sugary in the images of children that we have in Rousseau's *Émile* or Wordsworth's *Lyric Ballads*, the novels of Stowe or Dickens, Alcott or Twain should only remind us of the intense counter-energies of neglect and cruelty that these images are balancing out on the other side of the scale. Child labor in the 19th century would be only one element of this counterweight. Now, with the political and historical work of these images accomplished, the other side of the scale is empty and we are left looking at the sinking, overdone, too-insistent images that now offend us precisely because they have done their work and we no longer even remember the images that they were designed to correct. Freud's great work on the child at the end of the century concluded and liquidated a century-long task of representation that granted full psychic reality to the child: full experimental ordinariness. Rather than seeing Freud as the great demystifier of the many Little Nells and Little Evas, Alices in Wonderland, Tom Sawyers and Becky Sharpes, Little Men and Little Women, those Wordsworthian and Dickensian children that are so central to our critique of the failings of the Victorian imagination, we should see, rather, that in the tough-minded arrest of Freud's description of the violent, sexual, and jealous inner life of the child, there is only the final stroke of a process that is continuous from Rousseau to Freud, a process that includes, even in the case of Hawthorne's Pearl and Stowe's Little Eva, daring and expansive elements even where the sentimental flourishes are most evident.

Sentimentality, by its experimental extension of humanity to prisoners, slaves, madmen, children, and animals, exactly reverses the process of slavery itself which has at its core the withdrawal of human status from a part of humanity. As Stowe's original subtitle put it, *Uncle Tom's Cabin* is the story of a "man that was a thing." Within Christianity, sentimentality, and slavery were complementary tactics, the one extending, the other contracting the circle within which every

would also reach the maximum of sensibility or sentimentality, the maximum of complex sympathetic relations between people. Thus the subject of slavery and its representational strategy, sentimentality, have, in Rousseau's account, historical affinities rather than accidental literary connections.

The state of Nature—peaceful, independent, lacking in thought and feeling—has, however, one important inner state that Rousseau believes is the primary human feeling, one that is the root of all later feelings, or, rather, in the state of Nature there is a single exception to the self-interest that determines ordinary acts. This feeling is compassion and Rousseau describes it as a "species preserving" rather than individual preserving feeling. In compassion, therefore, humanity itself is at stake rather than the individual.

Compassion is, of course, the primary emotional goal of sentimental narration. Compassion exists in relation to suffering and makes of suffering the primary subject matter, perhaps the exclusive subject matter, of sentimental narrative. Rousseau offers an image for his idea of compassion that I wish to explore in some detail, because, in miniature, his image contains the primary psychology of sentimental narration itself and in particular the essential features of Stowe's treatment of slavery. His image is

> the tragic image of an imprisoned man who sees, through his window, a wild beast tearing a child from its mother's arms, breaking its frail limbs with murderous teeth, and clawing its quivering entrails. What horrible agitation seizes him as he watches the scene which does not concern him personally! What anguish he suffers from being powerless to help the fainting mother and the dying child.[11]

Because he is in the prison, the man's feelings cannot lead to action. Because the events do not concern him personally, the compassion is generous. It is, as Rousseau calls it, a species-preserving feeling as opposed to those feelings which have only the individual's own survival at their source.

In Rousseau's image there are four figures, but only three of them are given psychological reality. The oppressor is merely a wild beast, no further attention is given to his reasons or to his experience. Instead, the experience is given only for the three who suffer in different ways the violence of the beast. It is particularly important for sentimentalism that there be two victims rather than one, and that they be the essence of the family, mother and child tied by the quintessential bond of feeling, maternal love. The primary victim is not the child who undergoes physical destruction, but the mother who must be present when all that she values most is torn from her and destroyed. Even worse, she will survive the event and be marked by it permanently. It is separation and mental anguish that are the primary forms of suffering.

The imprisoned man sees not one victim but two: the child registers the maximum of undeserved physical suffering and the mother the maximum of mental suffering. But of course it is the destruction of the relation between the two that is primary and not the losses of either in separation. In the scene, where once there was a family, there remains only an individual who has lost everything. The compassion of the imprisoned man is a model for that of the reader who cannot leap into the print of his novel to save or prevent anyone and who does not himself stand to lose anything. The mother's grief in the scene is personal and self-interested. The prisoner's, because he loses nothing, is the best evidence of humanity itself.

The inability of the prisoner to prevent the suffering that he sees has several consequences. First, it makes him a crucial image of the reader of sentimental stories. A reader obviously cannot affect the outcome of events that he witnesses. Secondly, within the sentimental novel, it indicates the special importance of the child as witness. Little Eva who watches and learns the stories of the slaves is, because she is a child, unable to act to change what she sees around her. She is for that reason like the reader and the prisoner. Because she cannot act, she must suffer. She must, literally, die of the stories that she hears. The mysterious illness that carries her away is a symbol of knowledge itself, unendurable knowledge in the absence of the power to act.

The scene that Rousseau describes is a scene of parting. The child snatched and destroyed has been parted from the mother. Reunion is only imaginable in some other life. *Uncle Tom's Cabin* is, when broken down into its smallest units, an anthology of partings and forced separations. Slavery is, in effect, redescribed so that the reader sees it, not as form of labor, but as an ordeal of separations. In the opening chapters Tom is parted from Chloe, while Eliza and George part willingly so as to prevent their child being taken from them by force. In every scene of slavery in the novel, the ultimate event is the tearing apart of two people, husband and wife, mother and child, either for sale or for punishment. Like any writer of recurrent scenes, Stowe has to establish a gradation so that each successive scene or story can rewrite at a more extreme pitch the same formulaic facts.

On the boat taking Tom south, the slave trader Haley waits until the mother relaxes her attention for a moment, setting the child down so as to run to the rail of the boat to catch a first glimpse of the husband to whom, she has been told, she will soon be reunited. Haley snatches the child that he had sold without her knowledge.

> "Lucy . . . your child's gone; you may as well know it first as last. You see, I know'd you couldn't take him down south; and I got a chance to sell him to a first-rate family, that'll raise him better than you can." (144)

Hoping for one reunion, she has only exposed herself to one more parting. The results are carefully noted by Stowe.

> Dizzily she sat down. Her slack hands felt lifeless by her side. Her eyes looked straight forward, but she saw nothing. All the noise and hum of the boat, the groaning of the machinery,

mingled dreamily to her bewildered ear; and the poor, dumb-stricken heart had neither cry nor tear to show for its utter misery. She was quite calm. (145)

Later that night Tom witnesses her suicide as she slides over the side of the boat. The group on the boat has exactly Rousseau's configuration of four: The prisoner who witnesses but cannot act (Tom), the wild beast who snatches the child (Haley), the mother and the child. Since parting is an act of social death—Lucy is still a woman, but no longer a mother or a wife—the literal death of one of those parted is a crucial detail of both Rousseau's and Stowe's descriptions. The protracted death of Uncle Tom after his parting from Chloe is the physical ratification of his social death, which occurred with the loss of his family, cabin, and familiar world with which the novel began.

The two time schemes of sentimental stories involve moments when action is impossible: once an outcome is inevitable it is too late to act or to intervene, and, secondly, once an action is in the deep past and has left irreversible damage, even the consequences cannot be lessened, as they cannot be in the case of Prue, because one of the most serious results of deep experiential damage is the blocking of the power to have any new experience whatsoever, especially the kinds of experience that might balance or alleviate the damage. The tears that are so important a part of sentimentality are best understood in this context. Weeping is a sign of powerlessness. Tears represent the fact that only a witness who cannot effect action will experience suffering as deeply as the victim. For this reason stories of the long ago past play a central part in sentimentality: their only possible response is that of tears rather than revolt.

The most extreme suffering creates a ruin of the self, because the effects of the moment can never be repaired or balanced out by later joy. Rousseau's scene itself is a moment of forced separation—a parting—that will lead to a ruin; that is, to an old woman who will, many years later, have only this one story to tell. Partings and ruins, as I will show later, are the two temporal concerns of sentimental narration.

The most extreme form of parting is death, and deathbed scenes play a key role in the sentimental narrative. They are its primary image of domestic suffering. The reader of sentimental fiction participates in its moral purposes by accepting analogies between his own experiences of suffering and those of characters within the novel. For that reason the death of Little Eva is the most completely dramatized scene in Stowe's novel. Her death is both central to slavery and to the white reader's ability to imagine the consequences of slavery. The reader does so because he can make analogies from his own loss of a child or other family member in sudden, unexpected death—an experience that Stowe reminds the reader is nearly universal in the 19th century.

Deathbed scenes are experienced from the point of view of the survivors, not the phenomenal point of view of the one dying. Their subject is loss, not death. More precisely, their subject is separation that will be mended only by a later reunion in the after-life. Thus, deathbed loss is the only common experience that the white reader has that Stowe can use to comprehend slavery as separation, as the loss of members of a family who, like Uncle Tom, expect or hope for reunion just as the Christian reader does for his loved ones in heaven.

The importance of deathbed scenes depends, once again, on their involving action that occurs once a fate is inevitable but has not yet come to pass. A medical rescue is ruled out by the nature of the scene itself. The representation begins only when the death is certain. However, to use death as the central image for suffering is to strengthen the passivity within sentimentality. After all, slavery is a form of evil that we can imagine the world without. Slavery can be abolished, but, of course, not by a child like Little Eva. Death cannot be abolished or even mitigated as a permanent fact of separation, loss, and suffering. Therefore, where death is used as the analogy for social, remediable suffering, our general helplessness, like the helplessness of the child, the reader, or Rousseau's prisoner is underlined and the will to act is weakened if not denied. The feeling of suffering becomes more important than action against suffering. Tears become more important than escapes or rescues.

Partings staged around death rule out reunion, except in a religious vocabulary. The consequences cannot be undone politically. Tom cannot be ransomed back even by a lifetime of Chloe's work and saving. Once sold, he is dead, even if the fact takes several years to catch up to the inner reality.

The reunion that in Tom and Chloe's case can take place only in heaven, drawing therefore on the parallel that Stowe's reader of 1850 would feel to the promise for *his* family of such a reunion and such a psychological definition of "temporary parting" and separation, is actually staged for the reader in the subplot of the novel. Eliza, George, and little Harry are reunited by miracle after their separate flights.

The scene of this reunion is dreamlike and otherworldly. The Quaker household in which it takes place is the idealized mid-19th-century surrogate for heaven: an ordered, hardworking, generous, and principled family. The "New Heaven" of Stowe's picture is earthly and domestic. Its center, as is true in Dickens's "A Christmas Carol," is the abundant table around which a true family and its guests gather. In Dickens's England of employer and employee, a society of class, this must be a table at which Scrooge and Cratchett affirm an image of theoretical fellowship and reconciliation. For Stowe's America the table must have as its guest the black family, reunited by the combination of their own courage and the open help of diverse whites from every social level. At last, at the American table and within the idealized white family, the black family sits down as honored guests. As Stowe writes, "It was the first time that ever George had sat down on equal terms at any white man's table" (157).

Like Dickens, Stowe pictures the reconciliation as incorporation within a family around the table of abundance where there will be enough for all. But, also like Dickens, her narrative includes a constant reminder, focused by the presence in both stories of dreams, sleep, and unconsciousness, that this is an unreal and probably unrealizable solution. In fact, the reunion of the black family and the pious reconciliation between black and white that make that reunion possible are only a respite in the "flight" that is the true function of the counter-narrative of George and Eliza, the black family that parts itself rather than being parted by others, and can therefore reunite and seek a home where it cannot be parted. That home is neither Indiana nor Canada but Africa.

Although temporary, and with warnings built-in that it is utopian, Stowe's reunion is the central picture for what, in the Jeffersonian sense, is the promise of American life. Unlike Tom's Cabin, the home that he has but cannot live in, the Quaker settlement is the perfected image of a home. Stowe italicizes the word: "This indeed was a home—*home*—a word that George had never yet known a meaning for" (157). Chapter 23, "The Quaker Settlement," in which family reunion, racial reconciliation, the reality of home and the reminders of dreamlike fictionality and temporariness are all arranged as mutually necessary components for an image of American life without slavery, is also the chapter that concludes the first part of Stowe's novel. In the next chapter the scene changes to the boat headed for New Orleans and Tom's experiences in the urban St. Clare household. Like the death of Tom that concludes the novel and makes possible the heavenly reunion for which he will only have to wait until Chloe dies, this chapter includes a small symbolic death for Eliza.

Upon hearing the news that George is nearby and that she will be reunited to him that very evening, Eliza faints. She wakes up in bed, and from the bed and through her hazy consciousness, Stowe describes the heaven around her, the domestic heaven of the Quaker household.

> She opened her eyes in a state of dreamy, delicious languor
> . . . a strange feeling of security and rest came over her and,
> as she lay, with her large, dark eyes open, she followed, as in a
> quiet dream, the motions of those about her. She saw the door
> open into the other room; saw the supper-table, with its snowy
> cloth; heard the dreamy murmur of the singing tea-kettle; saw
> Ruth tripping backward and forward with cake and saucers of
> preserves. (155)

The scene continues in a ritualized way. Each sentence begins "She saw . . ." as though it were a vision or as though she had died and changed states, awakening in heaven. The six repeated phrases "She saw . . ." end with this passage:

> She saw them all at table, and little Harry in a high chair under
> the shadow of Rachel's ample wing; there were low murmurs
> of talk, gentle tinkling of teaspoons, and a musical clatter of
> cups and saucers, and all mingled in a delightful dream of rest;
> and Eliza slept, as she had not slept before, since the fearful
> midnight hour when she had taken her child and fled through
> the frosty starlight. She dreamed of a beautiful country—a
> land, it seemed to her, of rest,—green shores, pleasant islands,
> and beautiful glittering water; and there, in a house which kind
> voices told her was a home, she saw her boy playing, a free and
> happy child. She heard her husband's footsteps; she felt him
> coming nearer; his arms were around her, his tears falling on
> her face; and she awoke! It was no dream. The daylight had
> long faded; her child lay calmly sleeping by her side; a candle
> was burning dimly on the stand, and her husband was sobbing
> by her pillow. (155–56)

After her faint, Eliza half wakes and sees a world that is itself dreamlike but in which the black child has already been placed at the white table. Within this dream: she falls asleep. The sleep is a second small death after the faint. Now, at two removes, the dream of a black home occurs. Stowe's words "It was *no* dream" are in fact a statement of the opposite at the deep level.

But only at this moment and in this confused world between imagination and fact does the reunion take place. It does so, by a sharp act of staging, in the fundamental setting of the family and the center of the home: the bed. Only the next day does the reunited black family sit down to the table and a reconciliation, however temporary, take place by means of inclusion and abundance. Leaving her characters in this paradise, Stowe turns to Tom's story for three chapters before shattering the picture with the arrival of the slave-hunters and George and Eliza's resumption of their role as "fugitives."

By de-realising her own unique scene of reunion and reconciliation, Stowe reasserts that the story of George and Eliza is rightly the secondary story of her novel. Quaker values here stand for both the moral worth of the enclaves of all right-thinking energy and for the ultimate powerlessness of those enclaves within the overall society. Like a respite in time, a safe house in space is an exceptional and unstable reality. The atmosphere of death saturates the reunion scene. Beds are also the places for corpses and viewings. The candle in the dark room, the sobbing husband, the acts of fainting and falling asleep; the phrases in Stowe's description that speak of "one who has long been bearing a heavy load, and now feels it gone, and would rest" and the reiteration throughout of the strong word "rest" that feels more like the "eternal rest" of death than a reinvigorating rest that prepares for the "new life" that Eliza and George can now begin: every detail is used to evoke the contrary emotional account of this "happy" moment.

This heaven in Indiana is the America that might have been. The tidy cottage, in a small and neighborly settlement, suffused with kindliness, hard work, and the sufficiency that can always best be represented by food and the harmonious table of family and guests, translates the details of the Jeffersonian agrarian image of the heartland of America. The simplicity of Quaker wants guarantees no instability or greed. The rural economy will remain family centered and hard working. The moral and generous motives guarantee that material life will never itself become dominant. The community of the table and, then, that of the neighborhood, model the small-scale institutions on which the health of the larger, national institutions must be based. In the Jeffersonian image, the republic can be a healthy political entity only if it aggregates thousands and then millions of such self-sufficient and morally educative healthy units.

The homestead with its working family and freely held land is tied to other families by the informal and voluntary bond of "neighborliness." In America some traces of the Jeffersonian ideal are still felt in the unusual priority over more formal associations or political units of the half-familial concept of "neighbors" and the geographical unit of the "neighborhood."

The Quaker Settlement is the premise of the rest of Stowe's novel, and it is so because it repictures the privileged setting that the slave society has betrayed. The settlement is more an oasis from America than its smallest working unit. It is a rest house on a journey and not, as Jefferson had promised, the end of that journey itself. The analysis of slavery and of America itself in *Uncle Tom's Cabin* positions itself by means of the vanishing point provided by the reunion of one black family and their secondary welcome at one white table in Indiana. The need for this setting to be both heaven and earth, and for this scene to conclude the first third, but not the novel as a whole, arises from the fact that Jeffersonian America is now best represented, for Stowe, by the Cabin to which Tom will never return and not by the table loaded with the produce of rural hard work, independence, and abundance.

4. The Time Frame of Sentimental Action

In addition to the key facts of parting and ruins and the basic set of four characters, one further element of Rousseau's image requires emphasis. Rousseau describes the moment of destruction itself by means of the physical details of the act itself: "*tearing* a child from its mother's arms, *breaking* its frail limbs with murderous teeth, *clawing* its quivering entrails." The tearing, breaking, clawing, and quivering confront us with pure phenomenal acts taking place immediately in front of our eyes and having finality in and of themselves. They need no prior or consequential information to convey their horror or extent. Such phenomenal descriptions rarely occur within sentimental fiction because they violate its moral purpose in covertly identifying the reader with the aggressor, transforming the scene into one of violence rather than one of suffering.

In the representation of events, the time scheme of any one action is potentially infinite. Part of what we mean by a literary form like tragedy, sentimentality, naturalism, or the historical novel is how each excerpts highly ordered fragments of this undifferentiated duration to create meaningful action. The historical novel, for example, reaches back to create the moment of struggle between forces that in the reader's own day has already produced a decisive outcome. The struggle itself takes on the atmosphere of destiny.

The time scheme of individual events can include the entire life of the actor, the creation in childhood of the temperament that made the act possible, the circumstances in which the act was first thought of, the process of hesitation, doubt and choice and retreat just before the act is committed. This latter is the entire realm of time in which the act was possible but not yet inevitable and can be thought of as the second stage, after the diffuse stage of temperament when the specific act is not yet contemplated. The third stage is the relatively brief time in which on all sides the act is known to be inevitable but has not yet occurred. The fourth is the phenomenal moment of the act itself. The fifth is the brief time of immediate consequences and the sixth stage is the long-term consequences that are permanent and irreversible.

The time scheme of sentimental fiction represents events by means of only two of these six phases of action: first, the third stage, the brief moment after the event is inevitable, but before it has occurred; and secondly, the sixth stage, the event seen in the deep past by the single person most deeply and permanently marked by it. It is only in these two time spans that narrative relates events from the point of view of the victim and is therefore a record of suffering, rather than from the point of view of the oppressor and, therefore, a record of violence.

To return to the contrast between the modern and the sentimental versions of slavery: *Uncle Tom's Cabin* carefully narrates its events by means of the third and sixth time categories. The third is the anticipation of suffering and the sixth the deepest and most enduring consequences. On the other hand, *Nat Turner* registers only the first, second, fourth, and fifth temporal periods. Sentimental narrative avoids the roots of action in the past (the first and second periods) because all of our interest in these antecedents is aimed at understanding why the act occurred. It is made more reasonable and acceptable. By means of these phases of action we identify with the actor rather than the victim because, for the victim, such acts are unexpected. They have no antecedents and it is impossible to tell the antecedent life of a victim without making it seem as though that life brought about the event and thus the victim "deserved it." Only for the oppressor do such acts have a past. To give the narration a past is to recognize or implicitly adopt the point of view of the oppressor. In *Uncle Tom's Cabin* all the essential events occur suddenly. The novel begins with the slave buyer already signing the purchase for Uncle Tom. We begin once the act is inevitable, but has not yet occurred. By this means Stowe avoids interest in the motives or psychology of the oppressor, his hesitations, postponements, and alternative possibilities. All of this would humanize his act and make it forgivable to some extent.

The unexpected death of Augustine leads to Tom's second sale. Again we watch the event only from the moment that it is inevitable until it occurs. By making purely external catastrophes like sudden death or overwhelming debts cause the action, the causes themselves become systematic and uninteresting from the point of view of what motivated them and the reader is freed to become absorbed in the consequences for the victim. It is equally important that the narrative leaves out the short-term consequences in the picture of action because it is there once again that remorse, self-analysis, and compensation humanize the oppressor by means of his guilt or need for distraction. Narrative itself can embody the inner life of oppression by means of its form as well as by means of its content.

The second key narrative moment for sentimental fiction is the retrospective story of the deep past told by its still-injured victim. Wordsworth makes continuous use of this time frame and it is historically the fundamental time scheme of the ballad. In *Uncle Tom's Cabin* the story of Prue that Tom hears and then tells Eva is a typical case. So injured is she by what happened years earlier that she has fallen into self-neglect, stealing, drinking, and an indifference that seems to invite the ever more serious beatings of her cruel master until she is beaten to death. Just before her death she tells Tom of her children who were taken from her one by one, events no doubt forgotten by those who did them, whatever short-term remorse or compensating need for kindness they might have felt at the time. For Prue these events occur as stories exactly because they have primary reality to the victim and block out the possibility of any later reality.[12]

Similarly, the real consequences of Tom's sale occur when

his wife Chloe learns that he is dead, which, in being gone with little chance of return, he was, in effect, all along. Chloe hands over to her mistress the money that she had saved to buy Tom back, saying, "Don't never want to see nor hear on't again. Jist as I knew't would be—sold and murdered on dem ar old plantations!" (488).

By contrast, modern narratives eliminate all reference to the consequences in the damaged later lives of the victims and those whose lives are altered by the loss of the victims in those cases where they do not survive. They concentrate as *Nat Turner* does on the intensity of the moment itself with its grotesque or brutal details. All such representation is inevitably from the point of view of the oppressor rather than the victim because it is only for the oppressor that the act is climactic and hallucinatory in its physical reality. Thus, a writer like Kosinski in his novels *The Painted Bird* and *Steps* while pretending to write an indignant and traumatized historical account, in fact creates a surface of violence rather than of suffering and enlists the reader in the activity of savoring the pure surfaces of the present moment of action. The acts are without consequences that the reader ever sees and the victims are without antecedent personal identities that the violence interrupts. Thus he creates, as Styron and Capote did, a pornography of the events of violence in which the reader is invited into the pleasures of pure phenomenal action —the point of view of the oppressor.

5. EQUATIONS OF FEELING

The sentimental novel creates the extension of feeling on which the restitution of humanity is based by means of equations between the deep common feelings of the reader and the exotic but analogous situations of the characters. The 19th-century reader of Stowe's novel had no experience of having a member of his family suddenly sold off to a distant plantation from which he would never return, but the reader did almost certainly undergo traumatic, unexpected separation from someone, often a child, by death. The unexpected death of the only child, the center of a family's life, is, therefore, the experiential equation, dramatized in the death of Little Eva, by means of which the reader can cross over to the inner world of the slave family in which, without warning, a member disappears never to return.

The title of Stowe's novel uses this process of equation in a particularly subtle way. In the words "Uncle Tom" the title names its character from the point of view of the child. It is, of course, the children, often the white children like George Shelby or Little Eva who call him Uncle. He is not seen in the title as Shelby's Tom, a name that would refer to his reality as a slave, the property of his master. The relations of family are asserted over those of slavery. Throughout the novel slaves are not men and women, but brothers, sons, husbands, wives, daughters, and aunts. Their primary reality is relational and their names express this ironic fact.

However, the startling element of Stowe's title does not lie in the words "Uncle Tom" but in the cabin and the possessive letter "s." The title refers to Tom's ownership or possession of a thing. But, of course, it is Tom who is owned and governed by a possessive "s". He is the Tom of Shelby, rather than his own free-standing identity with first and last name, and that is the central fact of his identity. Still the title refers to him as the owner of a cabin.

That the cabin is mentioned in the title is odd because the cabin plays very little part in the novel. In fact the key detail is that, from the first act of the novel on, Tom no longer lives in the cabin and never returns there. It is therefore the place where he isn't, the home that he doesn't occupy, but to which all of his thoughts are directed as the home to which he would return if he could. The title therefore asserts his homelessness, his possession of a home that he has not yet reached. The emotional equation, here, for Stowe's reader, is to his own Christian image of heaven as the home to which he will return after a wandering on earth.

Slavery is by this means universalized within the Christian experience by means of the cabin that is our home precisely because we do not yet live there. A final important detail of Stowe's title ties it into the deep pattern of sentimental litera- ture. Many of the major sentimental narrative poems occur as meditations on an uninhabited place to which human reality can never be restored. Goldsmith's "Deserted Village," Words- worth's "Michael," and most of all, "The Ruined Cottage," which has so many deep connections to *Uncle Tom's Cabin*, are examples. In these narratives an observer stares at an abandoned or ruined habitation, calls up the life that was once there and tells one of those stories of decline and ruin that make human presence itself seem unsustainable.

Like deathbed scenes, the scenes of ruin deal with one of the two essential time units of sentimental narrative: the deep past in which loss has created ruins that cannot be repaired, nor can they be erased or forgotten. The half-finished wall in "Michael," the ruined cottage, Uncle Tom's cabin: these are places that testify to the human inability to prevail. Like all ruins, so important in the aesthetics of the sentimental period, they depend upon a historical sadness and define art as a permanent trace of human failure, the inverse of a monument.

Within sentimental narrative there are frequently characters who are themselves ruins. Old, exhausted, maddened by events that occurred long ago, they remain only fractionally alive, only alive enough to remember and retell what happened long ago, just as ruins do.[13] In Stowe's novel the slave Prue is such a ruin. Drunk, wishing only to die, ravaged by the sale of her children in a way that she can never repair, she is asked for her story by Tom, just as the physical cottages and cabins, walls and villages invite and even demand that their stories be told.

"Where was you raised?" said Tom.

"Up in Kentuck. A man kept me to breed chil'en for market, and sold 'em as fast they got big enough; last of all, he sold me to a speculator, and my Mas'r got me o' him."

"What set you into this bad way of drinkin'?"

"To get shy o' my misery. I had one child after I come here; and I thought then I'd have one to raise, cause Mas'r was n't a speculator. It was the peartest little thing! and Missis she seemed to think a heap on't, at first; it never cried,—it was likely and fat. But Missis tuck sick, and I tended her; and I tuck the fever, and my milk all left me, and the child it pined to skin and bone, and Missis would n't buy milk for it. She would n't hear to me, when I told her I had n't milk. She said she knowed I could feed it on what other folks eat; and the child kinder pined, and cried, and cried, day and night, and got all gone to skin and bones, and Missis got sot agin it, and she said 't warn't nothin' but crossness. She wished it was dead, she said; and she would n't let me have it o' nights 'cause she said, it kept me awake, and made me good for nothing. She made me sleep in her room; and I had to put it away off in a little kind o' garret, and than it cried itself to death, one night. It did; and I tuck to drinkin', to keep its crying out of my ears! I did—and I will drink! I will, if I do go to torment for it! Mas'r says I shall go to torment, and I tell him I've got thar now!" (240–41)

In sentimental narrative the work of art itself is the solemn memorial to the ruin, and the ruin is itself an inverse monument: a witness to human failure rather than to human glory or accomplishment. It is in this sense that the title names the empty cabin and the book itself, in which the story of Tom is told from the point of view of his death, is Tom's monument.

The melancholy of ruins, whether human or inanimate, depends upon the presence of the witness for whom the stories of suffering and of the failure to survive, stories that because they are deep in the past invite no compensation and provide no hope of redress, offer, instead, training in pure feeling and response. Such training lies at the heart of sentimental politics.

That feeling and empathy are deepest where the capacity to act has been suspended—as it is in the reader's relation to art—defines the limit of sentimental representation. But this amounts to a psychological fact as well as a cautious and questionable politics. By limiting the goal of art to the revision of images rather than to the incitement to action, sentimentality assumes a healthy and modest account of the limited and interior consequences of art.[14]

6. THE POLITICS OF SURVIVAL

The major paradox of Stowe's use of sentimentality rests on her moral use of the appeal to a universal human nature with primary feelings by means of which equations can be made from character to reader at the same time that she made use of an intensely analytic form of realism based on regions. Regionalism took the first steps towards the deterministic version of experience that we associate with naturalism. In regionalism, for the first time, the economic and systematic description of lives and experience moved to the foreground of realism. Each way of life, whether the life lived on plantations, the life of small frugal New England farms, or the risk-taking life of the pioneers generated, by means that could be studied and recorded, typical lives and life histories, characteristic and predictable tempers and outlooks, ways of dress and speech. Inevitably these details of character and action reflected the deep patterns of economics, work, geography, and climate. What we call naturalism is in fact only the final regionalism: that of the city with its far more desperate and magical life possibilities. Within Stowe's novel can even be found the Moral Darwinism of the competition for survival between regions: the conviction that certain forms of life were marginal and could not survive. Such life forms could not be selected because they were in contradiction with the fixed inner laws of human feeling. Other systems, compatible with those laws, would be found fittest.

In *Uncle Tom's Cabin* moral vocabulary, which at first seems grounded only in style and way of life, displays, finally, the imprint of regional economic and political forces. Here, what is at first glance the very element of behavior most tied to the novel of manners where customs, modes of speech and of thought define the surface of behavior in its many varieties of the cultivated and the boorish—as they do, for example, in the many regional styles found in such novels as Howells's *A Hazard of New Fortunes* and James's *The Bostonians*—are changed profoundly by Stowe's attack on an economic system, an organized and pervasive world of work and power. No longer are habits of speech and intellectual style merely personal or moral or picturesque. Instead, as would be true fifty years later in Dreiser or Norris, every turn of phrase has an inevitable and impersonal connection to the underlying economic system and its rationalization, mystification, or ironic and passive tolerance.

This systematic perception of styles of life is what outwits the picturesque and merely decorative tendency of local color and makes possible a profound set of variations on the universal human nature to which sentimentality is committed. Certain forms of life, and with them, certain underlying economic systems—obviously, that of slavery in this case—become suicidal and temperamentally deadlocked in the face of the few inviolable facts of family and feeling to which sentimentality with its enlightenment version of a common human nature is bound.

The greatest example of the force of this regional analysis comes in the central section of Stowe's novel where the deep structures of Southern temperament are outlined in their decadence and in their self-contradiction. What we at first see as the easy-going, ironic, aristocratic charm of St. Clare undergoes deepening and reversal again and again under the pressure of Stowe's analysis. This central section is her clearest claim to structural genius and offers the most profound analysis of the South as a region in American literature before the work of Faulkner.

It is St. Clare's whimsical, easy-going generosity that leads him to buy Tom as a "gift," a toy, really, for Little Eva. It is this light and ironic touch that guarantees that Tom will be mildly treated. As Stowe will say later: in New Orleans Tom's chains were hidden within flowers.[15] Slavery seems almost a game or a way to make the lives of Tom, Topsy, Dolph, and the others more pleasant and genteel than they otherwise might be. This easy-going master allows the disorder of the kitchen, the small lies and thefts of the servants, the comic parody of his valet, and all of these seem the fruit of a surplus of wealth too great, of time too ample for the minor details of work that have to be done.

The moral vocabulary of this region is first challenged by the alternate vocabulary of Ophelia to whom all of this is what she calls "shiftless,"[16] a word that Stowe uses for the primary "sin" and evil of all evils for the moralistic, orderly, blunt New England spirit. This word "shiftless" maps out the very same facts as the term "aristocratic leisure," which is the goal of a slave economy and the basis for such higher activities as the hunt, the reading of novels, witty conversation, flirtation, boredom, and drinking. Shiftlessness and leisure are the same events framed in the language of regional perceptions and moral geography. Just as one section of the country creates the character type of the "Southern belle" and another that of the refined and industrious "young lady" out of the same biological facts, so too each system generates a predictable set of names for experiences, names that install or defend what we, then, take to be reality.

The style of household management was at the center of moral order for New England: neatness, parsimony, the daily round of tasks were themselves a key element of moral uprightness as they never can be in a world of servants.[17] Discipline, thrift, self-reliance: all of these are sheltered within the judgment that the Southern household is "shiftless." The New England virtues grew out of the soil of equality, the disdain for servants, and the economy of household self-reliance. Those of the South are a visible mark of a plantation system of household servants and its consequences.

Stowe deepens her account by testing each system in its primary social task: the raising of children. The education of Topsy from savage to free human being by Miss Ophelia, the failed education of the violent and rash cousin Henrique, and the furtive self-education of Little Eva who dies of the learning that she, unlike her parents, cannot ironize or deny: these three educations are the central matter of Stowe's middle section. With education the moral consequences of honest rigor, on the one hand, and easy-going charm and grace, on the other, are tested at their decisive point. As Albert says when looking at the wild, petulant, and violent child Henrique

> "There is no doubt that our system is a difficult one to train children under. It gives too free scope to the passions, altogether, which in our climate are hot enough. I find trouble with Henrique. The boy is generous and warm-hearted, but a perfect fire-cracker when excited. I believe I shall send him north for his education where obedience is more fashionable, and where he will associate more with equals, and less with dependents." (300)

That Albert mentions climate as an element of temperament means that Stowe is aware, as she is throughout her novel, that the systematic description of moral life depends on what the naturalists later would call "forces"—climate, inheritance, and economic system. Her intelligence about the causal relationships within this three-part system is notable. Climate produces or invites an economic order of a specific kind, which, in its turn, produces temperament and moral character. As she says earlier in her novel when speaking of the Shelby farm in Kentucky:

> Perhaps the mildest form of the system of slavery is to be seen in the state of Kentucky. The general prevalence of agricultural pursuits of a quiet and gradual nature, not requiring those seasons of hurry and pressure that are called for in the business of more southern districts, makes the task of the Negro a more healthful and reasonable one; while the master, content with a more gradual style of acquisition, has not those temptations to hard-heartedness which always overcome frail human nature when the prospect of sudden and rapid gain is weighed in the balance with no heavier counterpoise than the interest of the helpless and the unprotected. (9)

This is an awareness unmatched in American literature until Naturalism fifty years later.

Immediately after her analysis of education, which leads to the harshest judgment against St. Clare, a reversal leads to a deeper defense. St. Clare speaks of the choice that every master must make in the system of slavery between a violent, brutal imposition of order and an easy-going tolerance of a corrupting kind. Suddenly, as the alternative to violence, his neglect seems the better moral choice. However, a final turn is given to moral styles by the test of Tom's freedom. After promising the dying child Eva that he will free Tom, St. Clare puts off the actual legal act in his easy-going way. His confident ease tells him that there is no need to act in an urgent and hectic way. Tom is lost to Simon Legree because of this final expression of leisure and charm. On the other hand, Topsy is saved by Miss Ophelia, who sits St. Clare down and insists, against his protests, that in her disciplined, New-England style of legalistic firmness she will have him sign over Topsy to her on the spot in a binding transaction.

In the stages of Stowe's representation, what begins as picturesque regional differences of manner slowly reveals itself as systematic and almost Darwinian strategies of survival within the moral geography of various systems. The strategies of the Southern female's infantile helplessness, her narcissism and preoccupation with her own imagined illnesses and sufferings are represented as a necessary form of moral noise generated to overwhelm the visible and genuine sufferings of the slaves who surround her. Such lives are the final stage for those who like Marie "from . . . infancy had been surrounded by servants who lived only to study her caprices" (173). The adult life that follows has its typical pattern.

> A life of constant irritation, bodily and mental—the friction of ceaseless ennui and discontent, united to the ordinary weakness which attended the period of maternity—in course of a few years changed the blooming young belle into a yellow, faded, sickly woman, whose time was divided among a variety of fanciful diseases and who considered herself in every sense the most ill-used and suffering person in existence. (173–74)

The death of Eva, the subsequent impulsive death of St. Clare, the sale of the slaves and the return of Marie to the infantile pleasures of her parental home where she will be forever kept in a pampered childish existence: these conclusions disintegrate the moral system under which the family and slaves lived. The system dies of the habit of concealment which leads finally to the family's disbelief in the serious illness of Eva. The system dies equally of the mystified perceptions and moral vocabulary which they are compelled to employ, the styles of grace and carelessness that they are compelled to practice by the nature of the economic life that they have constructed. A region in which slaves must be seen as "selfish" and "lazy," where masters can pity themselves as the "victims of their slaves, even the slaves of their slaves" (187), or, on the other hand as the ironic beneficiaries of one form of evil among many inevitably different, but finally, similar, evil social systems—such a world has set in place a self-canceling variation—like a non-surviveable Darwinian mutation—of a universal human nature that will, in the end, have its revenge.

3

The Life History of Objects:
The Naturalist Novel and The City

The description of Chicago that Dreiser gives early in *Sister Carrie* could stand as a description of America itself in 1890.

> In 1889 Chicago had the peculiar qualifications for growth which made such adventuresome pilgrimages even on the part of young girls plausible. Its many and glowing commercial opportunities gave it widespread fame, which made of it a giant magnet, drawing to itself, from all quarters, the hopeful and the hopeless—those who had their fortune yet to make and those whose fortunes and affairs had reached a disastrous climax elsewhere. It was a city of over 500,000 with the ambition, the daring, the activity of a metropolis of a million. Its streets and houses were already scattered over an area of seventy-five square miles. Its population was not so much thriving upon established commerce as upon the industries which prepared for the arrival of others. The sound of the hammer engaged upon the erection of new structures was everywhere heard. . . . Streetcar lines had been extended far out into the country in anticipation of rapid growth. The city had laid miles and miles of streets and sewers through regions where, perhaps, one solitary house stood out alone—a pioneer of the populous ways to be. There were regions open to the sweeping winds and rain, which were yet lighted throughout the night with long, blinking lines of gas-lamps, fluttering in the wind. Narrow board walks extended out, passing here a

house, there a store, at far intervals, eventually ending on the open prairie.[1]

The confidence that leads the city to this gigantic sketch of its own future compels the present to live in the near-empty outline of what will someday be real. The combination of bravado and forlornness that makes up the mood of Dreiser's picture has elements of late 19th-century Impressionism, the sadness of Whistler, and early 20th-century tough atmospherics, the bleakness of Hopper. In his image of the streetlights on all night and blown about by prairie winds with not a house yet in sight, Dreiser invents a feeling of the pathos of the future that is complementary to the nostalgia or regret that are the traditional forms of the pathos of the past. His Chicago has both the confident vitality of persons or places that know they have a future, and the unreality of the resulting fact that, seen from the point of view of the present, actual life is nearly empty.

The Chicago that Dreiser describes is a mediating term. It is simultaneously a synecdoche for America, of which it is the most compact and representative part; and, on the other hand, it is a metonymy for Carrie whose small, future-oriented self with its plans and expectations extending out into reality like trolley tracks and strings of gas lamps, the surrounding city magnifies and gives a concrete expression to. Throughout the late 19th century the privileged setting of the city gained energy from this double role of synecdoche and metonymy. The London of Dickens, the Paris of Baudelaire, the St. Petersburg of Dostoevsky, the Chicago of Dreiser—in every case the miniaturization of social and political fact is superimposed on the magnification of deeply interior psychological states. Both are made simultaneously concrete by the same urban details. Uniquely for America, these facts are those of incompleteness, anticipation, and what I will call "practice." By practice I mean the way in which what appear to be present actions are in fact only real when considered in relation to a future for which they are the preparation. The rehearsal of a play or a football practice are each indexed to a future moment. Dreiser uses the central symbol of the theater in *Sister Carrie* for the reason that, since even the performance, once it finally takes place, is an unreality, a semblance, the practice that preceeds it is a far deeper unreality, and is therefore not even a "real" moment of unreality; this translates for him into a complex account of social practice in general and the consequences of living in a future reality.

The city mediates between and models the larger society, once that society is understood as an economy, and the individual, once that individual is understood as a career, a self-projection. This world of ambition and possibilities favors a strong capacity for dreaming and often creates a confusion between dreaming and lying since both are forms of impatience with the present. In *Sister Carrie* these two near actions are isolated: Carrie is a dreamer, Hurstwood a liar. In her essay "Truth and Politics" Hannah Arendt asks the question whether, since politics has its orientation towards the future, that is, towards states of being that are not yet actual, it is not by its very nature hostile to the truth since truth accounts for the features of the actual present. Politics, in her account, has a natural affinity for lying because, like lying, politics wishes the present were different from what it actually is. What Dreiser calls yearning, and what we can see saturating his novels in the variety of forms of dreaming, acting, lying, and practicing is thus a form of politics in Arendt's sense of the word. Politics, in this very broad meaning of the sketching of the future along with the commitment to that sketch to an extent that implies that one has already accomplished a mental departure from the present, is the quintessential personal and public activity of the economic world that Dreiser describes as the heart of America.

The city which provides a transcription of this economic and future-saturated world is a more intimate and a more concrete privileged setting than either the wilderness or the

Jeffersonian setting of Yeoman farms. The wilderness did not give a synecdochic account of society because once settlement and society were in place the wilderness vanished. The wilderness is a subjunctive setting. The wilderness was the prehistory whose spirit and costs could be traced in the history itself. Similarly, the Jeffersonian pastoral dream of an America of independent and contended farmers was a contentious, argumentative image, always at war with the actual, ongoing development of America into first a commercial, then a manufacturing, and finally into an urban society. It was a consoling or an indicting counterimage to the real. Neither the wilderness, nor the Jeffersonian setting could therefore embody the larger social reality since each was, in very different ways, designed as an alternative to it. The half-built city was the first literal image. Paradoxically, what was literal about it was its unreality. It was not yet there; it wasn't yet itself. The wilderness was, even in its invention, the home for escapees and rebels like Thoreau and Natty Bumppo. The Jeffersonian setting, as in the Quaker household in *Uncle Tom's Cabin*, was a sanctuary from, not a faithful account of, a larger social world. The Dreiserian city was a perfect fit, both representing the psychological dynamics of the individual and the politics of America itself. In Dreiser's two great novels, *An American Tragedy* and *Sister Carrie*, the internal logic of the American city was set in place.

1. THE CITY AND THE TRANSLATION OF DESIRES

What is the city from the inside? What is around one when the city, around the body like a second, more spacious suit of clothing, is experienced in use? In every direction are the terminal points of desires. Buildings are never brick, aluminum, or glass—which they might be if considered part of nature—but restaurants, churches, brothels, shoe stores, apartments, offices, and factories. Buildings translate into places the desires for food or God, sex or various coverings, shelter or work. Both desires and buildings exist in numerical ratios that enact the intensities of the psyche. The number of churches per square mile can be compared to the number of bars or bookstores or brothels. Frequencies exist for the desire for shows or the desire for food. Statistically, any city gives a map of the psyche, a quantitative account of the strength and complexity of the system of human desires at a given cultural moment. How much provision for sitting and watching, how rare and peculiar the variety of flowers or prostitutes for sale, how large the living rooms of apartments (how complex the desire for family life) compared to public spaces for entertainment; how many places where one can be alone for at least ten minutes, how difficult the access to prayer—the city is the visible account of the balances and imbalances of the psyche. In the city to look at any "thing" is to glance through it at once to the desire it records and services. Streets and sidewalks: metonymy for our desire to be "there." A church: metonymy for what piety or prayer we feel. Factories and office buildings: metonymy for the element of work, with the appearance of such buildings translating our feelings about work. The city is the metonymy for our total system of desires. Things within the city have lost substance, what "they" may be is a kind of film over what we can see as our own want. A bicycle, a cake, a bed—these are not things like snow, a star, a bird's call. Even what trees remain are now translations of our desire for shade, for the color green, for the illusion that we retain a comforting link to the earth.

Far from being in any simple way estranged in the city, man is for the first time surrounded by himself. In every direction is a mirror, every sound is an account of his affairs. All that disappears vanishes because he no longer cares for it; all that comes to be enacts his desire. Unlike nature where other laws than human desire, other patterns and appearances drive man into himself as a haven, where in every case man experiences his life set within an other to which he only fugitively corresponds, within the city anything outside the body is there only because it was projected there by will and need. Baudelaire who first developed the art of seeing through the so-called objects of a city with a glance that undid their history back to the human hand, the human reason for being there, could look even at ships in the canals to see

C'est pour assouvir
Ton moindre desir
Qu'ils viennent du bout du monde.[2]

Sailors and ships, storms at sea: what is all this about but the pinch of pepper we wanted on our food and sent ships 12,000 miles to find? The ship is a metonymic substitute masking, as every physical object masks and maps within the city, this energy of desire. Further, it was Baudelaire who developed the motifs of voyaging and walking the streets—these motions within the city—as the metaphors for the acting out of desire. The self-experience and recognition reached earlier by thinking is, under the conditions of the city, obtained by shopping. The display of goods behind a glass that we cross in fantasy defines the process of yearning, choosing, and imagining the transformations of the self by things, by others, and by places that the city proposes. In the single greatest sequence of scenes in *An American Tragedy*, Clyde and Roberta shop for death, for an abortion, and having no sense of world or market, Clyde begins in the only store he knows well, a men's clothing store. He interrupts the clerk selling him ties to press him about where he can buy an abortion, then continues his shopping in drug stores, and finally in a doctor's office.[3]

Within the city all things become commodities—all objects, all other persons even shade, company, learning, or religion. They are commodities not so much because they are desired and sold, but because our relation to them has shifted from that of caring for things that one has (whether given or bought) to buying things one hasn't. Commodities, objects within the city, are not property. They are not valued for the way I finally can absorb them into my life—this can be done with only a few things that I must care for, keep over time, entangle with the experiences of my memory. No, the idea of property is irrelevant and we often feel suddenly indifferent to things once we get them home or to places once we have voyaged there, as Proust described. We are bored with them, wish them used up so that we might replace them. With property a person absorbs a thing into his life. Instead we seek to be absorbed temporarily into the magical life of the things. We expect to borrow from them. The vitality of objects in the city—what Walter Benjamin called the "sex-appeal" of objects—is generated by the style and atmosphere that they propose to us.[4] As an economic system the city is a market for the rental of aura, or to use Dreiser's word, atmosphere.

The effect of being surrounded by objects, places, and persons that rent out being is to create around the body, everywhere one looks, the materials for fantasy and dreaming. The dreamer within the city is its character, as the shepherd is *the* character of the pastoral world. In Dostoevsky or Dreiser, in Joyce's Bloom or Zola's Gervaise, this absorbing fantasy around the self, this abstractly possible experience haunts and dwarfs what remains of the actual. All such characters walk and dream. For the dreamer, this shepherd of the city, who walks within this world of translated desires, his experience of himself is no longer tasted in solitude, by withdrawal, as one earlier withdrew to a position over against the natural world and society to take the measure of himself. For a man inside the city his self is not inside his body but around him, outside the body.

Since I mean this literally I will try to make this idea more plausible before showing its force with *An American Tragedy* and *Sister Carrie*. Memories, secrets, feelings, the interior chatter of the mind—the whole realm of what we call "privacy," all that is not deliberately made available to others or is given at our discretion, all that could be moved from place to place with me or that would survive being cast-away, as in the Crusoe myth, all that I would find myself left with if the world were annihilated except for my body—this residue was in the age of individualism what was meant by the self and was located inside the body. It survived deportation. Now, it is one of the most interesting facts about the representation of modern characters in Zola or Dreiser that this territory of the self within the body has vanished or declined in interest or investment. Some readers find the characters in Zola or Dreiser "empty" or uninteresting because they either lack this territory or their author is indifferent to the state of our knowledge about it. Dickens was the first to omit this sphere that we call "consciousness," and he was the first, along with his contemporary Baudelaire, to discover the maps for the empire of the self within the city. The primary setting of the dreamer is the street.

We do not have to agree with the absolute quality of Andre Breton's striking statement that the street is "the only valid field of experience,"[5] to accept the fact that, as a spatial frame, the street has a central value in city experience. Its qualities of the accidental and the temporary, its invitation to a varied and multiple attention, its courting of adventure and interruption and its presentation of a number of partial events within the same field of vision so that anyone can, while carrying out his own action, watch or scan a variety of disconnected acts: all of these suggest that the open space of the street is the antithesis of the room—that classic space of drama and the novel, with its fixed and interrelated set of characters, its single unifying action and its consecutive development. From at least the time of the *flaneur*, the disorder and perceptual shock of the street were sought for their own sakes, developing in Baudelaire's prose poems a literary form suitable in its momentary qualities of action, mood, surprise, and mystery.

The architectural historian Benevolo, whose *History of Modern Architecture* is now the standard work, describes the

aesthetics of this experience as it can be found for the first
time in Impressionist Painting.

> Impressionism grasped the character of the urban scene more
> clearly than any of the critics or writers of the time: the
> continuity of its spaces, all inter-connecting, each open to the
> next and never enclosed within a single self-enclosed frame of
> perspective, the fact that it was composed of recurrent identical
> elements, qualified in an ever-changing way and therefore
> dynamically in relation to the surroundings, the new relation-
> ship between the architectural frame, which was now indefinite
> and unbounded and the traffic of men and vehicles, the renewed
> unity between architecture and the street, and in general the
> sense of the landscape as a dense mass of objects all equally
> important but perpetually in a state of flux. . . . The greater
> or rather the total openness of these painters to every natural
> or man-made object restored the unity of the landscape which
> had been broken by the industrial town; nevertheless the in-
> tensity and emotional involvement typical of the realists was
> lacking and in its place was a sort of detachment and im-
> passivity.[6]

What Benevolo calls detachment and impassivity is described
from another point of view, that of the sociologist Simmel as
"reserve" or the "blasé attitude," a typical and psychologically
necessary survival device against the solicitations of attention
and concern in the city that are too various and demanding to
be accommodated.[7] Simmel describes the response to these
solicitations as one in which the intellect, in order to protect
the deeper layers of the personality, becomes the dominant
faculty sent out to receive and sort the swarm of experiential
episodes. Simmel's essay of 1905, "The Metropolis and Mental
Life," had an extraordinarily wide effect on the sociological
theories of the city that follow. The Chicago School of Park
and Wirth began out of direct study with Simmel.[8] Walter
Benjamin's studies of Paris and Baudelaire are deeply indebted
to Simmel and are in many places a restatement of his work.

Spengler's treatment of the city in his *Decline of the West* uses all of Simmel's primary categories. The more essential work of Weber implicitly follows the psychology of Urban Experience first described by Simmel.[9]

Louis Wirth was adapting Simmel to the American scene when, in his classic essay "Urbanism as a Way of Life," he wrote, "the contacts are brief, impersonal, superficial, and segmental. The reserve, the indifference and the blasé outlook which urbanites manifest in their relationships may thus be regarded as devices for immunizing themselves against the personal claims and expectations of others."[10]

Although as a terrain of experience the street called up such specific forms of representation as the prose poem and the urban form of Impressionist Painting, far more important than the seeking out and collecting of street experiences is the architectural and technological attempt to make the characteristics of this experience available indoors or at home, that is, to give to our rooms and enclosed spaces many of the qualities of spatial experience for which we have developed a psychological attraction in the field of experience of the street.

The great department stores of the late 19th century created the crowds and the possibilities of observing and connecting open-ended glimpses of action and drama that resettled the world of the streets indoors in a glamorous and spatially exciting setting. Benevolo's description of the space of the street draws on his earlier description of the dramatic and novel indoor space of the London Crystal Palace Exposition.[11]

More important than these public and commercial spaces is the transformation of the psychology of domestic and familiar experience brought about by the introduction of the open floor plan within modern architecture. The open floor plan of the modern house, which we usually associate with Frank Lloyd Wright and the set of houses that he designed in the Midwest between 1890 and 1910 soon became the standard for domestic space. Rudolf Arnheim has described these houses as creating an outside space inside.[12]

What the open floor plan encourages is a variety of actions and tasks taking place within sight of one another. While one person cooks, another reads, the children play, and each is aware of the others in an intermittent way. Each interrupts the other from time to time. Concentration on any one thing is segmented, and distraction is a natural and pleasing element. By eliminating the walls and doors behind which cooking or reading, conversation or play took place, the open floor plan lent itself to a psychology in which concentration or attention gave way to a moment-by-moment multiple focus. Corridors and transitional spaces are eliminated. The increasing use of glass, one of the more essential spatial facts about modern buildings, permits the felt presence of the outside to mix with the inner world.

These features of the urban world that reach their fullest expression in the arena of the street draw their importance from the novel structure of experience that they make possible. The American map of this structure, recorded in terms of acting and murder, which are in effect two routes towards an identical extinction of the traditional self, was invented by Dreiser in his two great novels of the city, *Sister Carrie* and *An American Tragedy*, novels in which he achieved for the city as a privileged setting exactly what Cooper had done for the wilderness. Dreiser invented the figures and the motifs by means of which the city became visible as a cultural fact in America.

2. TEMPORARY WORLDS

The opening scene of *An American Tragedy* leaps into new territory of the self in as striking and profound a way as the scene of the *petite madeleine* in Proust. A seedy little band is walking the streets, perhaps a family, but not enacting themselves as family. They are "the man-in-the-street," omitted in the attention of others who, likewise walking, scan or muse in the way one does as a "passerby" in the absence of events that solicit attention. Suddenly the band stops, two adults, four children. This is nowhere, no place. Suddenly it is a place they make up as they begin to sing. Now it is an improvised church, on the spot, and in singing they become ministers and choir, the passerby, their attention now solicited, must choose to become or refuse to be the congregation, audience, members of this half-hour church. In the middle of nowhere they have improvised a world, temporary, voluntary (only they accredit themselves "ministers," each person in the congregation is a self-appointed instant member of this church). On the spot a social structure exists with roles and tactics forced into existence under what seems emergency conditions: as someone might decree, "For tonight this square of sidewalk is my bed," or as someone can find himself in a storm and transform what was a moment before "newspaper" into "umbrella."

This fragile, ad-hoc world transforms itself again, now into a business. The congregation is asked for money, is sold tracts. This is, after all, how these people get their living. Now each one in the congregation must contribute or refuse to "support" these people. The half-hour service ends, the congregation transforms itself into walkers by drifting away, becoming "the man-in-the-street." The ministers and choir move on, becoming walkers. The place becomes nowhere, no place again. No trace, no "evidence" as the book will later name all traces of the past, remains. The experience, the roles, the physical reality of the church within which each lived for half an hour, dissolve.

No role exists unless it is honored like paper money in the eyes of others who must, in order to validate my role, not simply approve or permit, but enact a complementary role. They must become co-performers. If all passersby lower their eyes and walk on when a man begins to preach in the streets, they rule by their co-performance that he is performing the role of madman, not that of minister. Without the co-performers no one is anything at all. They are passersby.

The tactics for being someone under emergency conditions, conditions that are permanently temporary, fragile, improvised (without any prestructuring past), and absolutely dependent on the cooperative enactment of others, these are the essential tactics of identity in the city world of *An American Tragedy* or *Sister Carrie* where the profession of actress names this general condition precisely.

In choosing to begin with Clyde "in place," performing, but resentful of a squalid, theatrical self-enactment, Dreiser abandons the comforting sentimentality of the innocent central character. Typically, the novel of adolescence depends on an outsider who sees such structures first as an observer, then makes up himself by choosing among them. Such outsiders have a self that they invest with social position, career, and wife, usually in ways that express or publicize the nature of that self. In Dreiser no outsider exists, no innocent. Clyde begins in state, experiencing what was for Nietzsche the characteristic feeling of western civilization—resentment. Every motion of his life compounds flight and desire, neither feeling exists even for a moment except in the presence of the other. As the motion of desire is given in the metaphor of shopping, so its opposite is generated literally with more and more overt force in the book; Clyde flees his family (metaphorically); he runs from the auto accident (literally); after the murder he becomes a fugitive (totally absorbed in flight).

Bluntly put, within Dreiser's novel the question of authenticity never exists. Clyde has no self to which he might be "true." Literally, he is not yet anyone at all. For the calm or even frantic possession of himself Clyde substitutes an alertness to the moods of others, to their "take" of him. By the end of the book the lawyer's projection of the jurors' take, designs every gesture Clyde will make. Ultimately, Clyde lives in their moods, borrows their being, as he had earlier borrowed Gilbert's appearance, until we have to say he is more often them than himself. So attentive is he to his observer that he springs to life as a reflection of what the observer appears to have seen. He gets his "self" moment by moment as a gift from the outside. He murders by imitation (after reading of a drowning in the newspaper) as he loves by imitation (his being mistaken for Gilbert).

Throughout the novel Clyde is in motion towards or away from worlds he does not merge with. Fleeing or yearning, running or shopping, seducing or aborting, saving money to buy, planning to do, hoping for—"if" and "if only," could he only . . .": Dreiser begins hundreds of sentences with these words. The two motions to embrace and to murder, possess and amputate are sharpened and magnified by the staircase plot. With each turn the circumstance is wider, the matter more ultimate, but the same matters are, with each new circle, once again in view. Finally, at the same lake he seems ready at once to snatch at the social world he most desires and annihilate the clinging world from which he cannot be free.

Nowhere in Dreiser's novel is there the slightest trace of society, as that word is understood in nineteenth-century novels. Instead there are worlds, like the world of the Green-Davidson Hotel, the social world of the Giffiths, the world of condemned prisoners at the penitentiary, the shabby rural world Roberta comes from, the sexually languid world of the girls who work for Clyde. These worlds are islands of varieties of aura, some glamorous, some contaminating. Everyone in Mrs. Braley's rooming house appears to Clyde to be from "the basement world." He speaks of the "better atmosphere" of the Union Club in Chicago. No distinction expresses the fact that whereas he *lives* in the rooming house, he was a servant in the Union Club. The atmosphere soaks in equally. In the city all aura is translated into places, and the moments of entering a new atmosphere, whether of the restaurant the bellboys visit on their night off, the living room of the Griffiths mansion, the death row, or the dyeing room of the factory—these are among the most perfectly crafted moments of Dreiser's novel. Places supplant manners. In communities, in societies, manners were the codes of behavior, often most precise in speech and language, encoding deference or intimacy, reserve, as-sumption or condescension—codes of behavior that enact the rules of presence, the way in which we enter or situate our-selves in each other's experience. Places in Dreiser give out this social grammar once located in behavior, in manners, in the implications of conduct.

Zola was the first to abandon society as the object of public representation for the new post-social topic of "worlds." How-ever, in Zola these islands have economic and systematic integrity based on work: the entire world of the coal mines in *Germinal*, the world of land and farming in *La Terre*, the military world of *Le Débâcle*. Each is a rational sector of experience, known by the array of types, the kinds of language or experience, the appropriate modes of sexuality, humor, pride, and violence. Public, permanent compartments of so-ciety, they imply the larger, total society even while the mag-nification Zola applies, the isolation of spheres, makes them seem absolute. The food world, the art world, the sex world of *Nana* are all paradoxically still within a world, although courtesan, artist, grocer are monomaniacally absorbed in their sectors of work.

For Dreiser the worlds are neither economic, nor public, nor are they permanent centers of activity. Worlds are not generated by the webs of work, because in Dreiser work itself is only one kind of atmosphere, enthralling to the bellboy of the Green-Davidson Hotel, contaminating to the worker in the "basement world" of the collar factory. Work is just another place where one is seen by others and fixed by their looks that melt self and atmosphere together. Dreiser's worlds are temporary, magical improvisations like the little religious world on the street, or the perfectly named "Now and Then Club" through which Sondra engineers her flirtation with Clyde and his entry into the social set. Every boarding house is a world, the hotel bellboys have their own world of nights out at restaurants and brothels or outings in the country. Even the condemned man, Clyde, and his two guards on the trip to Auburn prison make up a world performing itself for the crowds who gather to see the now-romantic murderer. The guards feel honored and proud (as Clyde once felt walking with Hortense) to be seen with the murderer. His aura gives them identity: they are "the murderer's guards" with a genitive construction as potent as the erotic genitive Clyde feels for "his beloved's breasts." Murderer and guards form one aural body as Clyde working at the Green-Davidson is a limb of one aural body that includes guests, employees, furniture, renown, position in St. Louis, and lights.

So many fragile, transient worlds exist in Dreiser's novel because the root meaning of world here is anything outside the body that, if seen by another, contaminates or glamorizes the self. When Clyde walks with Hortense she decorates him, testifies to him. Two lines of energy contribute to the power of worlds to share being, to lend identity: the first is the force of collective identity, the second, the magic of places.

Collective identity in the novel is more substantial than individual identity. Being "one of" the Griffiths or "one of" the Green-Davidson bellboys or "one of" the prisoners condemned to death, is a more precise matter than being Asa Griffiths or Ratterer or even Clyde Griffiths. The novel describes "sets" or bands, clubs or cliques. Many of the sharpest representations in the book are of days Clyde spends within a precise identity set. Dreiser brilliantly records the life of groups, factory workers moving through the streets to work or the camping trip of the social set. He is remarkably indifferent to kinds of life that cannot be described as ongoing—activities or groups that one "joins."

Experiencing oneself as "one of" this or "one of" that is the primary way of constituting a self in the novel. The material is outside the body in sets. "He felt he would like to caress her arm. . . . Yet here he was a Griffiths—a Lycurgus Griffiths —and that was what now made a difference—that made all those girls at this church social seem so much more interested in him and friendly" (I, 210). Or again: "He danced with her and fondled her in a daring and aggressive fashion, yet thinking as he did so, 'But this is not what I should be doing either, is it? This is Lycurgus. I am a Griffiths here. I know how these people feel toward me'" (I, 213). The perfect concision of identity: I am a Griffiths, *Here*. I am a bellboy, here. I am a condemned prisoner, here. These are the absolute figures of identity: collective and limited by that terrible word *Here*. Both set and setting are around the self. Dreiser notes that the old death row was literally a row with all the cells side by side so that the prisoners never saw one another, never saw the "Them" that each was "one of." In the new death row—to Clyde's fastidious distaste—the cells face and the men become a hysterical, visible set acting out in front of each other variations of their common fate and identity. Architecturally, the state of New York has taken account of the new conditions of self by making the setting enforce a set.

The first act of looking at someone in the book is to look *around* him. Clyde feels humiliated to know that as the eyes of others come to focus on him in the street the "around" that they notice first is the shabby religious family that he must wear like an irritating garment. Because the savor of worlds replaces the savor of individual character within the body, Dreiser designs a web of metaphors to represent this new condition. Clyde often wears a uniform, the first metaphor of "set" identity. First as a bellboy, later as a servant at the Union Club, then as a businessman, finally as a prison inmate. Uniforms designate both sets and one specific place within a setting, as in a resort hotel the casual clothes of the guests define their places, the formal uniforms of the elevator operators, theirs.

More profound than uniforms is the territory Dreiser calls "manner," a stylized, collective tone of behavior. After a time in the Union Club, Clyde, though a servant, takes on the aloof, sexless manner of the successful businessmen there. Manner is absorbed, not learned. The power of adopting a manner depends on an interior blankness over which many colorations can pass. In court Clyde's attorneys coach him in a manner, and when shaken he must look to the eyes of his lawyer whose return look will recall him to what he is supposed to be.

A more brilliant device of collective identity than either uniforms or manner is the resemblance between Clyde and his cousin Gilbert. The blur between the two identities creates the entire plot of the novel. Because Clyde has the manner of the Union Club and is first seen by his uncle Samuel within its civilized aura, and because he resembles in a striking way the manufacturer's son Gilbert—a double "rented" being—he is invited to Lycurgus and given a job. Again, Sondra Finchley offers a ride to Clyde, having mistaken him for Gilbert; then begins her flirtation with him and opens society to him. She continues, at first, only to irk Gilbert, to strike at Gilbert by taking up his neglected cousin. It is only because he can so easily be "taken for" someone else that Clyde can exist in Lycurgus as "himself."

Identity, blurred or collective, externalizes the question of who I am, converts it into the question, Who do they take me for? Who does it look like I am to them? A stunning scene enacted again and again in the book could be called "looking around to see who I am." At the collar factory Clyde approaches the secretary guarding the door.

> "Well?" she called as Clyde appeared.
> "I want to see Mr. Gilbert Griffiths," Clyde began a little nervously.
> "What about?"
> "Well, you see, I'm his cousin. Clyde Griffiths is my name. I have a letter here from my uncle, Mr. Samuel Griffiths. He'll see me, I think."
> As he laid the letter before her, he noticed that her quite severe and decidedly indifferent expression changed and became not so much friendly as awed. (I, 184)

After his capture people come to see him and he sees himself in their eyes:

> Their eyes showed the astonishment, disgust, suspicion or horror with which his assumed crime had filled them. Yet even in the face of that, having one type of interest and even sycophantic pride in his presence here. For was he not a Griffiths—a member of the well-known social group of the big central cities to the south of here. (II, 162)

Dressed as a prisoner, his hair cut, he sees himself as others might:

> There was no mirror here—or anywhere—but no matter—he could feel how he looked. This baggy coat and trousers and this striped cap. He threw it hopelessly to the floor. For but an hour before he had been clothed in a decent suit and shirt and tie and shoes, and his appearance neat and pleasing, as he himself had thought as he left Bridgeburg. But now—how must he look? And tomorrow his mother would be coming—and later Jephson, or Belnap, maybe. God!
>
> But worse—there, in that cell directly opposite him, a sallow and emaciated and sinister-looking Chinaman in a suit exactly like his own, who had come to the bars of his door and was looking out of inscrutable slant eyes, but as immediately turning and scratching himself—vermin, maybe, as Clyde immediately feared. There had been bedbugs at Bridgeburg.
>
> A Chinese murderer. For was not this the death house? But as good as himself here. And with a garb like his own. Thank God visitors were probably not many. (II, 348)

A magnificent scene. Dreiser at a moment like this has no equal. Clyde imagines the "other" and then finds him out there as another version of himself. The Chinaman is the first installment of his "set" which he accepts by reminding himself: that's what I am *here*, in this setting. He ends grateful to be invisible. In miniature this scene recapitulates the curve of the book, and its sinister constituting glance that destroys, the glance of the Chinaman, is the world glance returned when Clyde looks around to see who "I" am.

On the street singing hymns he is wounded by "who" the bystanders take him to be. In court the eyes of the jury take him to be a murderer. The sexually vital girls he meets at the church social take him to be a Griffiths, and Clyde knows well the difference between being taken to be one of the Kansas City Griffiths and one of the Lycurgus Griffiths. Contaminated or magically ennobled, in either direction he is a blank center engulfed by worlds.

Often the aura of a world is precisely located in a building, a space that becomes a metonymy for that world. The Green-Davidson Hotel in Kansas City where Clyde works as a bellboy is evoked with rapture and desire. The hotel has more being, more reality than anyone within it. To each it rents out a part of its self so that the pale creatures become "someone who works at the Green-Davidson" or "someone staying at the Green-Davidson." Clyde looks at the Alden farm or the Griffiths mansion and sees them as "selves," as what could be taken for his self by others were he within. He shudders or feels exhilarated, threatened, or tempted by them in that intimate way most people feel only about *actions*. We feel honored or shamed by what we have done because, in our sense of self, what we *do* expresses and announces what we are. It is the one transmission from the portable, interior self. In Dreiser, this decisive burden of *actions* is taken over by settings. The two fundamental settings are clothes and the slightly larger garments that we wear called houses or rooms. Both are the first elements of the self around the body. The Griffiths' factory makes collars, an article of clothing. All of Clyde's money goes into clothes, a more widely visible self than one's room or house which one must leave behind much of the day. Decisive clues against him at his trial are his two straw hats, his clothes and suitcase. Hortense offers to exchange sex for a coat, and in one of the greatest of Dreiser's scenes, Clyde goes in desperation to a clothing store to learn from a clerk selling him ties where he can locate an abortionist.

Clyde is never intimately sculptured by his actions. He does not seem to do them. Every decisive event in his life is an accident, a mistake, or a confusion. In the existential sense, he does not "do" his life. For that reason his acts are not essential to who he is. He seems peculiarly absent at the most decisive moments, such as when an auto accident kills a child. To Clyde, Roberta dies by accident, really, and what was he in the boat but "someone" holding the camera she bumped her head against? He does not participate in what he does, but he does participate in where he is. These places index who we must take him to be, and they can be found outside him, while the accidental moral life of his acts goes its irrelevant way within. Being here and not there has replaced doing this and not that.

As a pun the word "place" suggests physical space, social station, and occupation at the same time. But for all the desperate importance of worlds and places within worlds, Clyde is never seen at home. He seeks admission or flees confinement, he desires and flees; worldless. The two haunted spaces of the novel where Clyde enacts his life are hotels and water. He begins work in a hotel, lives in the small-scale hotels that are rooming houses, finishes his life in the state-run hotel known as a prison. His outing with the bellboys and Hortense takes them to a hotel in the country, and before Roberta's death they go from hotel to hotel in the resort area. A hotel is an ideal home, like the street church with which the book begins, for improvised, overnight worlds.

Yet hotels *are* worlds. The Green-Davidson in Kansas City has a dense, alluring presence in spite of its changing cast. Dreiser can sketch in precisely the "world" of each of the rooming houses Clyde lives in—their manner, their tone, their place in the scale of society. Because they are worlds there exists a kind of visual rule to judge who does or does not belong there: who is, as we say, "out of place" there. The acute vision of the book does not rest with situating Clyde in transient, improvised worlds, temporary worlds, but in representing him as fundamentally worldless, unable to "belong there" even in temporary worlds. At the end he is dead, not of justice, nor of social revenge, but of a new disease: worldlessness.

Within every world there are defective positions, reserved for those who are deeply "out of place" there, who don't belong, but are permitted to be on the spot if they agree to admit in some clearly announced way that their case is an exemption. The servants at the Union Club are poor boys permitted to bask in the aura of the club, sharing its dignified manner, treated with the civility of all relations there, even to be seen as part of this world—as Clyde is first seen by his uncle Samuel—but at the cost of signifying by their uniforms that they are there by permission and don't in fact belong. They participate in aura without membership in the world. This is Clyde's social place at every moment in the book. When invited to the Griffiths' mansion he can come only at the cost of their constant reminders that he is a poor cousin, there on tolerance as an act of kindness. In the social set that he cannot afford Sondra slips him seventy-five dollars so he can pretend to pay their way, and the money itself is his stigma. Even when he descends to a world, in the menial work of the factory, he is seen there as exempt since, as the nephew of the owner, he may suddenly no longer be a fellow worker but a boss. With the Griffiths set he is an outsider, but in every other set he is equally an outsider because the others see him as a Griffiths. Every world is doubled by his presence inside it.

On his first day at the Green-Davidson Hotel Clyde is called to Room 529.

[He was then . . .] sent to the bar for drinks . . . and this by a group of smartly dressed young men and girls who were laughing and chatting in the room, one of whom opened the

door just wide enough to instruct him as to what was wanted.
But because of a mirror over the mantel, he could see the party
and one pretty girl in a white suit and cap, sitting on the edge
of a chair in which reclined a young man who had his arm
around her.

   Clyde stared, even while pretending not to. And in his state
of mind, this sight was like looking through the gates of
paradise. Here were young fellows and girls in this room, not
so much older than himself, laughing and talking and drinking
even. . . . (I, 44–45)

Clyde sees the scene of youths like himself but mysteriously
different, privileged, worlded, but he sees it in a mirror
glimpsed through a crack in a door someone holds almost
closed against him. His uniform and purpose there are the
distance for which the slightly open door is a metonymy. He
sees only an image, a fiction in the mirror. Later in the novel,
the newspaper is this mirror. Clyde, with touching innocence,
tells Sondra he has been following the social life of her set "in
the newspaper." He reads in the newspaper of a drowning at
a lake that gives him, in his empty resentment of Roberta, a
crime that he can imitate. And in a stroke of grotesque bril-
liance, Dreiser has Clyde's mother support her trip east by
acting as a reporter for a newspaper, writing up the sentencing
to death of her own son!

   The newspaper or mirror is a periscope in the novel, feeding
images from worlds to other worlds. The newspaper is a
metonymy for the world hunger Dreiser associates with the
city, the torment of proximate worlds that one can never
enter, turned into a self-torment by reading about even more
fantastic, unavailable worlds.

   Clyde enters always with a talisman or trick that simultaneously admits him and curses him: his uniform gives him
the glimpse of the hotel paradise, his resemblance to Gilbert
tickets his entry to Sondra and her set, the slipped seventy-
five dollars pays his way into the camping vacation.

The most perfectly orchestrated scene of defective membership that marks Clyde throughout is his joining the campers
after the murder of Roberta.

> For although met by Sondra, as well as Bertine, at the door of
> the Cranston lodge, and shown by them to the room he was to
> occupy, he could not help but contrast every present delight
> here with the danger of his immediate and complete destruc-
> tion. . . .
> If only all went well, now,—nothing were traced to him! A
> clear path! A marvelous future! Her beauty! Her love! Her
> wealth. And yet, after being ushered to his room, his bag
> having been carried in before him, at once becoming nervous
> as to the suit. It was damp and wrinkled. (II, 123)

These "althoughs," "ifs," "if onlys," "and yets" are the permanent structure of his doubled world, every world becomes
conditional, concessive, possible, yet in becoming possible,
impossible. For the very same reason the door is opened, a
foot is held against it to open it only a crack.

That Clyde is askew within every world is demonstrated in
his helplessness when he tries to connect within a world. He
does not know how to find an abortionist because he belongs
neither to the middle-class world whose doctors accommodate
when a "problem exists" (as we learn from the attorney's
story) nor to the working-class world where lore and gossip
would supply him with the name of a back-alley abortionist.
His life being arranged with mirrors, he has no connections
anywhere and ends up in a clothing store desperately trying
the clerk's knowledge of "solutions." Later Dreiser carefully
shows that were Clyde of the Griffiths world the entire crime
would have been hushed up. On the other side, were he an
ordinary factory worker no one would have cared. Because
the jury can resent him as a well-connected seducer of a poor
girl while the Griffiths deny him as "not really one of us," he is

important enough to exterminate but not important enough to rescue. Justice, through the choice of lawyers and legal maneuvers that Samuel Griffiths can buy for Clyde, is a matter of sets and worlds, too.

What is his name? Clyde Griffiths (of the Kansas City Griffiths)? Harry Tenet (his name during his flight after the car accident)? Clyde Griffiths (of the Lycurgus Griffiths)? Clifford Golden or Carl Graham (the names he uses to register at hotels with Roberta)? At his trial the evidence against him consists of matters of identity. How can he explain his two straw hats, the wet suit? His is the first murder in literature in which the weapon is a camera. Dredged up from the lake it contains identifying pictures that along with Roberta's letters that he forgot to burn turn the jury against him decisively.

In *An American Tragedy*, defective membership means not only having no world but also having no self. Deprived of set and setting, having no group which we can say he is "one of," Clyde drifts into the inevitable worldless acts: murder and then execution. Unable to erase the signs of his set through abortion or murder he is caught halfway through the door and imprisoned on the threshold. Literally, death row is such a threshold since the men there are no longer legally alive but not yet dispatched. Like the sidewalk church with which Dreiser began, it is a temporary, self-contained world of fixed roles under emergency conditions. The ever stronger meaning of the adjective "emergency" as we move from the improvised church, to the emergency of abortion, to the flight after murder, to death row suggests the inner nature of what Dreiser means by tragedy. For him tragedy has a circular or spiral quality where each return to what seems to be the same predicament is in fact located farther from the center. The tragic account that he created in the 1920s is less complex and less profound than the neutralized, half-tragic, half comic account present two decades earlier in *Sister Carrie*. In fact, it is the earlier novel that is structured around the city itself in its entire range of possibilities, and in that novel Dreiser invented his most striking vocabulary for the urban privileged setting.

3. MOTION AND BETWEENNESS

Recalling the white mirage of the Chicago World's Fair of 1893 twenty-five years later in his *Autobiography*, Henry Adams wrote, "Chicago was the first expression of American thought as a unity; one must start there."[13] At the Chicago Exposition, which marked that city's coming of age, one of the major attractions was the invention of the engineer George Washington Gale Ferris, a wheel 250 feet in diameter that raised fairgoers in tiny cabins high into the air to let them view the fair as a whole. Ferris's wheel played the part in the Chicago Fair that had been played in the previous French World's Fair of 1889 by the famous tower of Dr. Eiffel.[14] This amazing and useless momument that commemorates only itself and the beauty of structural metal capped the career of one of the greatest bridge builders of the 19th century. The Eiffel Tower is, in effect, a bridge with only one end fastened to the earth, completing the promise that many of the breathtaking 19th-century bridges had seemed to offer that someday a bridge would be built that would dispense with the idea of coming down. Eiffel's tower operates as the bridge builder's dream of linking the earth and the sky as two banks of a great river of air. It is the technological representation of the transition between the bridge and the airplane, which at that moment was the just-about-to-be born marvel that would extend the bridge's power to leap over space rather than passing through it, turning any two points on the earth into piers of a bridge that is now a small moving metal object.

Dr. Ferris's wheel Americanized Eiffel's amazing bridge by bending it into a circle and setting it into motion. It is a bridge that begins and ends at the same point with the bridge itself now moving rather than the person. It is, therefore, even closer to the airplane and provides for its riders who leave the earth in a little cabin, rise into the air and return for a landing, a kind of practice for the as yet non-existent experience of an airplane ride. This economical circle that joins the pleasure of rising and the fear of falling into one repeatable smooth motion became at once a feature of every carnival and amusement park in America and continues to be the central identifying symbol, like a cathedral spire seen at a distance marking a medieval town, of the presence of a carnival or fair.

The mechanization and knowledge of motion that created the assembly line, the McCormick Reaper, the automobile, and the Ferris Wheel along with hundreds of other inventions on the same principle in late 19th-century America has been exhaustively studied in Sigfried Giedion's *Mechanization Takes Command.* Giedion notes that, just as all technological facts become at some point miniaturized and domesticated as a way of enjoying what in other contexts might be frightening or oppressive in its novelty, an increasingly popular American object domesticated and routinized the steady motion of work, turning it into a lulling relaxation. That object was the rocking chair.[15] The rocking chair permits one to rest and move at the same time, canceling the effects of motion by allowing it to recur in the same fixed spot. The rocking chair on a porch—that quintessential American image—permits the rocker to be in motion and yet never to leave the same place, to be outside the house and yet still in the domestic space, to participate in street life without leaving family safety, to enter the world and yet to be protected from it by the porch rail and the inevitable picket fence at the sidewalk. The state is one of striking in-betweenness, as though a way had been found to factor out the pleasures of many conditions and fuse them while discarding all of the inconveniences that generally accompany either motion or rest, domesticity or sociability, family life or citizenship.

The rocking chair, like the Ferris Wheel of which it is a small domestic arc, displays none of the linear motion of progress and exploration but rather the fact of rising and falling. The world of Dreiser's *Sister Carrie* is composed of images of motion of which the most profound are not the horizontal motions of train rides, carriage excursions, trips to Europe and walks on either Broadway or the Bowery, but instead the tragic and vertical motions of rising and falling: the motion of the rocking chair. The wealth of motion in the novel insists that the society itself is, by means of its new streetcars, railway systems, steamships, carriages, and endless places to walk, most itself when in motion. Dreiser's novel begins with Carrie and Drouet flirting on a train approaching Chicago. Its second half begins with a rhyming scene that has Hurstwood and Carrie on a train to Canada and then New York. The novel ends with a train approaching New York carrying the Hurstwoods to a steamship for Europe. Travels are proportional to wealth. A trolley ride to work is the shortest trip, impossible for Carrie for whom a four-dollar room and board plus sixty cents weekly trolley fare exceeds her salary of four dollars and fifty cents by ten cents. The final trip to Europe is the longest. Hurstwood, we see, is the only driver, first taking Carrie on a carriage ride in Chicago and later learning to drive a streetcar in New York. Drouet is a traveling salesman on the train routes of the Midwest. Characters walk around all day looking for work: Carrie when the novel begins, Hurstwood at its end. Once employed, like Carrie in the Chorus Line, they march back and forth on the stage to earn a living or sit, as Carrie also does, punching holes in the shoes that move too rapidly past her on the work line. Entire classes of men have become "tramps" and "drifters," their very names implying constant motion. This society for its pleasure rides out in carriages just to "take a ride" or it promenades on Broadway. Of all of these motions, some of them circular, many of them fixed by tracks, and almost all of them forms of living in which one is "Carried" along, as Sister

Carrie's name implies, none so dominates Dreiser's novel as that of Carrie again and again rocking in her chair by the window. On her first evening in Chicago, and in our final glimpse of her in her suite at the Waldorf, she sits and rocks at the window. The window substitutes for the porch, enabling one to see the street as a spectacle, a performance, without participating in even those controlled ways that a porch makes possible. A window theatricalizes experience both for the one rocking on the inside as well as for the passerby who glances up and sees the "pretty scene" of a young lady wistfully rocking at her window in the evening light.

Dreiser notes that in Chicago at the time of *Sister Carrie* plate-glass windows were for the first time being installed at the street level by businesses of all kinds. These windows turned the work inside into a show designed to play out the operation of the business for the chance spectators who were passing.

> The large plates of window glass, now so common were then rapidly coming into use, and gave to the ground floor offices a distinguished and prosperous look. The casual wanderer could see as he passed a polished array of office fixtures, much frosted glass, clerks hard at work, and genteel business men in "nobby" suits and clean linen, lounging about or sitting in groups. (16)

The windows turn activities into scenes or photographs, but as Dreiser says at the end of his description, the effect of these windows was to "overawe and abash the common applicant, and to make the gulf between poverty and success both wide and deep" (16). The window creates a polarized world of inside and outside, actor and spectator, rich and poor that would not occur if what were going on inside were simply unknown. All scenes become opportunities for self-classification in that they seem to invite you in and invite you to imagine being in while strongly reminding you that you are out.

4. THE ANTICIPATED SELF

The windows that convert reality on both sides to enacted scenes are consciously used by Dreiser to define a state of the self in motion that we might call the self in anticipation. When Drouet first takes Carrie out to eat he "selected a table close by the window, where the busy rout of the street could be seen. He loved the changing panorama of the street—to see and be seen as he dined" (55). The performance of dining in which passersby become one scene and those they, in turn, glimpse for a moment through the glass another is only the outer shell of an action that repeats itself across the table between the two diners, host and guest.

> Drouet fairly shone in the matter of serving. He appeared to great advantage behind the white napery and silver platters of the table and displaying his arms with a knife and fork. As he cut the meat his rings almost spoke. His new suit creaked as he stretched to reach the plates, break the bread and pour the coffee. He helped Carrie to a rousing plateful and contributed the warmth of his spirit to her body until she was a new girl. (56–7)

The performance of serving food that converts objects into setting and props and somehow animates even his rings until they seem to speak, results in transformation of the spectator: Carrie becomes a new girl as his spirit enters her. This meal is the first stage of her seduction and leads to the flight from the Hansons, her taking on of the role of "Mrs. Drouet" (without of course going through the technicality of marriage), and then leads Mrs. Drouet into the role of Carrie Madenda, the stage name that permits her to play the role of Laura in the Elks Club performance. This final role, like the initial dinner, she is able to do only because Drouet comes backstage almost to hypnotize her into confidence. He enters her soul with his gregarious exuberance and, in effect, possesses her from one side in order that she can, from the other side of her being, be possessed by the role and feelings that she must simulate in the drama of Laura.

The windows beside which Carrie rocks or eats with Drouet are also used by Dreiser for his central description of the sources of her vitality. When Hurstwood begins to fall in love with her, Dreiser pauses to describe the inner source of the depth of feeling and spirituality that allures Hurstwood. He finds it in certain scenes:

> Her old father in his flour-dusted miller's suit, sometimes returned to her in memory, revived by a face *in a window.* A shoemaker pegging at his last, a blastman seen through *a narrow window* in some basement where iron was being melted, a bench-worker seen high aloft *in some window*, his coat off, his sleeves rolled up . . . (132, emphasis added)

Her connection to these worlds is what gives her a spiritual side that makes her attractive to Hurstwood, "a lily, which had sucked its waxen beauty and perfume from below a depth of waters which he had never penetrated and out of ooze and mould which he could never understand" (132). The waters too deep for Hurstwood are only a slight transformation of what is for Carrie a window: hardened water through which she always sees the other side of toil from which she stems and from which she has only luckily escaped. The windows look back into this world of origins only once. Their normal role is to reveal the future world of anticipation and possibility. On her first night in the shabby little flat of her sister and Hanson, Carrie, after writing a letter to Drouet, "drew the one small rocking chair up to the open window and sat looking out upon the night and streets in silent wonder" (14).

The anticipatory motion of rocking previews and practices the actual later flight from the apartment. Carrie's anticipation resembles the anticipation of Chicago itself. "It was a city of over 500,000 with the ambition, the daring, the activity of a metropolis of a million" (15). The streets and trolley lines have already been built out into the prairies in anticipation of houses that will not be built for many years. Streetlights go on and off along these streets where there is not yet either danger or safety. When Hurstwood takes Carrie for their first ride it is out along the New Boulevard, five miles of "newly made road" with not a single house yet built. The road is *made* in the sense of "made up" because it connects only two parks. It is an anticipatory place for Hurstwood's first anticipations of an affair with Carrie. The vocabulary of speculation, whether economic, civic, romantic, or professional is so compelling that Drouet's first praise of Carrie's acting ability drives her to her rocking chair by the window where it "was as if he had put fifty cents in her hand and she had exercised the thoughts of a thousand dollars" (145). The psychological notion of down payments, installment credit, and commodity speculations is here entirely in place in the inner world.

The anticipatory world has as its consequence a state of the self preoccupied with what it is not. Carrie's friend Mrs. Hale has as her pleasure a drive out in the afternoon, "to satisfy her soul with a sight of those mansions and lawns which she could not afford" (106). At a higher level of the same world, Mrs. Hurstwood, who lives in one of those very mansions, cares only about, "that little conventional round of society of which she was not—but longed to be—a member" (80). Carrie herself lives with the Hansons while longing for the life represented by Drouet, only to get Drouet and long for the life represented by Hurstwood and in turn to get Hurstwood only to long for the life represented by Ames. Even the Hansons toil and save in their little flat because they are saving up to build a house on the two lots on which they have already paid a number of installments.

The anticipatory self has as its emotional substance hope, desire, yearning, and a state of prospective being for which the notion of acting is merely a convenient cultural symbol. Dreiser very carefully differentiates acting from deception. Carrie acts, Hurstwood deceives. He withholds from Carrie the fact that he is married, then tricks her into leaving Chicago with the lie that Drouet is injured and needs her help. He withholds the fact of his theft, tricks her into a sham marriage and finally lies to her about jobs and prospects that he has just around the corner. Acting, in other words, is not sham, but rather a form of practice. Carrie, while living with Drouet, practices in her mirror the gestures that she has heard him praise in other women. She imitates the graces of the railroad treasurer's daughter until she becomes worthy of the role of "Mrs. Drouet," and, in time, worthy of Drouet's better, Hurstwood. Acting draws its moral meaning not from a world of true and false but from a dynamic society where all are rising or falling. Chicago, as Dreiser first describes it, is a city of "the hopeful and the hopeless—those who had their fortune yet to make and those whose fortunes had reached a disastrous climax elsewhere" (15). This is a world of "might-be" and "has-been." The only excluded possibility is full present being. Deprived of the present, each is saturated with either the future or the past. Each is defined by prospective being and the acting that practices the yearned-for role, or by retrospective being for which Dreiser's image is the newspaper and the compulsive reading that Hurstwood, once fallen, uses to keep track of the things he has lost. The newspaper is always about yesterday.[16]

A device that marks the self in relation to the future or the past in selective ways is the mobility of names and epithets in Dreiser's novel. Carrie is Sister Carrie, Carrie Meeber, Cad, Mrs. Drouet, Carrie Madenda, Mrs. Murdock, and Mrs. Wheeler as well as Laura, Katisha the Country Maid, the frowning Quakeress, and her many other roles. Hurstwood becomes Murdock and then Wheeler, demonstrating the difference between aliases and stage names. In his final name, Wheeler, he is motion itself, a wheel broken loose from a carriage that continues to roll only as long as the path is downhill. He becomes a drifter, a walker of the city, a street-car driver, a loosened wheel. Opposite him is Carrie who is also literally her name, carried on the tides to her fame. Beneath these no longer stable social names are the many epithets that more accurately describe persons precisely because they name roles. Carrie is called "Drouet's little shop girl," or "the little drama student." Drouet is "the drummer" and Hurstwood "the dressy manager" until, after the theft and his flight he begins to be called, resonantly, "the ex-manager." From then on he can never be free of this retrospective name that defines him only by what he is no longer—by his "has-been" status. When he imagines taking a new job, a humiliating future and a lost past squeeze out the unnamed present: "Bartender—he the ex-manager!" (311) Or when asked: "'What is your name?' 'Wheeler,' said Hurstwood" (370). Even when Hurstwood is learning the new role of streetcar motorman so that he might appropriately be called "the new motorman" (a future name) or "the scab" (a present name), Dreiser writes: "The *ex-manager* laid hand to the lever and pushed it gently, as he thought" (373). The purchase on either the future or the past is locked in by means of names that aim the self either upward, if it is rising, or downward, once it begins to fall. The names are, in effect, frozen verbs. Manager, actress, driver, drifter, and salesman are nothing but disguised verbs that describe managing, acting, driving, drifting, or selling. In the same way Carrie and Wheeler are named in only a thinly disguised way for the passive act of rising and the activity of decline.

The force of these epithets arises as one side effect of the use of acting and the theater as central institutional facts in Dreiser's description of the new American world. Proper names are multiplied until they vanish. As the newspaper reports, "The part of Katisha the Country Maid will be hereafter filled by Carrie Madenda" (394). She in turn is only playing the part of Carrie Madenda in the theater. In her neighborhood she is Carrie Wheeler who has the stage name Carrie Madenda in order to play the role of Katisha. Beneath the layer of the neighborhood, she is in fact unmarried: Carrie

Meeber playing Mrs. Wheeler who has the stage name Carrie
Madenda for the role of Katisha. The theatrical language
invites us to consider all social life as "parts" and "roles." Wife
and salesman, drifter and sister, all take on the temporary and
fictional aspect of parts that are studied and then performed.

5. WORK AND ROLE: ACTING

In the Chicago half of his novel Dreiser creates a hierarchy of
work that rises to more and more directly involve selling the
self while at the same time providing a sanctuary for the self
within the more clearly acknowledged fictionality of its role.
At the bottom of the scale are jobs in which the self is
extinguished by toil. Carrie begins by actually making shoes
—the poor man's train, carriage, and steamship, his only
technology of motion. Her father, whom she pictures covered
with the white flour of the mill where he worked, is the perfect
illustration for the extinguishing of the self by the toil that
produces such goods as flour and shoes. Hanson, who is the
image of a lifelong toiler, is a silent man described as "still as a
deserted chamber" (48). At the next level above these toilers is
the salesman Drouet, connected to objects by selling rather
than making them. He handles only "samples" and is not
fatigued by the weight of things. What he sells is really himself,
his exuberance and pleasure-loving confidence, but as in all
sales of this kind a trick occurs at the last moment. The
customer who has really bought the salesman finds that in
fact he has bought a set of brushes, an encyclopedia, or a
vacuum cleaner. The art of sales is the elision of the self and a
product throughout the selling process, lending the salesman's
personal glow to the object, then the severing of the connection
after the completion of the sale so that the customer is left
with only the object.

One step above Drouet is Hurstwood who, while a salesman,
has no object to sell. As manager he, in effect, sells his tone,

his presence and air to the nightclub. Standing around, the "dressy manager" rents out his personal approval. Objects have disappeared from the selling process, but the fictionality of social role is increasing. The customers do not *buy* Hurstwood, they purchase the right, by talking to him and being acknowledged by him as worth talking to, to believe that they are his equals. What Hurstwood sells, therefore, is not his personality, as Drouet does, but his air of knowing and making available the entire circle of which the customer would like to imagine himself a member. Drouet's personality and vitality would survive disconnection from the machinery of social life. Unemployed, Drouet would still be a lively and sought-out man. Because Hurstwood sells only his tone and services as an intermediary between figures in a circle, once severed from the social machine he is, as Dreiser says of him in New York, "nothing."

At the peak of the hierarchy of work that Dreiser has constructed is the actress. Her self, her inner emotional being, is what is sold to the ticket holders. The objects have vanished entirely. The personality and vitality alone remain to sell. Yet, this final identification of self and work is carefully regulated by the fictional shelter of the stage role: Laura, Katisha, the frowning Quakeress. It is only in Drouet that the actual self is naively present and in balance with the objects that it sells and separates from itself in the act of selling. With Hurstwood, self and the fiction of position; with Carrie, self and the more profound split between self and role make more naked the renting out to others of the self, while sheltering the self within a "part." The world of New York is free of shoes, flour, and salesmen with their samples. The economic world is object-free. Transportation and entertainment, moving and acting are all that remain: motorman and actress. In Dreiser's Chicago hierarchy the two poles are paradoxically similar. At the bottom as a result of toil the self is exhausted by the objects that it produces, drained by shoes, covered with flour. At the top the self is not extinguished but fictionalized and costumed. The flour that covered Carrie's father is replaced by the stage makeup that covers his daughter.

What Dreiser has seized upon in his careful ordering of the world of work and its relation to the self is the privileged role of acting and the theater that had since the beginning of the Romantic Period been seen, on the one hand, as the central institution of the city and, on the other, as the most serious challenge to the romantic theory of the self. In the Seventh Book of Wordsworth's *The Prelude*, London, a world of performers, orators, ecclesiastical and political actors, and street performers like the blind beggar, has at its center the theater and the tumultuous fair. Wordsworth is only one of a set of 19th-century writers and artists that would include Poe, Baudelaire, Zola, and Manet to name only a few, for whom the theatricalization of life in the city made the theater or that theater of ordinary life, the street, the central spiritual fact about urban life. It is, however, in Rousseau's *Letter to M. D'Alembert On The Theatre* that the most profound analysis of the theater in its relations outward to the community and inward to the self is recorded. Rousseau's *Letter* has been explored by Lionel Trilling in his *Sincerity and Authenticity* and Trilling's main ideas deserve summary.[17]

Rousseau's concern is to denounce the theater and to prove its incompatibility with any acceptable and moral community. He sees three interconnected factors: (1) republican virtue, (2) the position of love in society, and (3) the sharp contradiction between the social role of women and their appearance on the stage as actresses. In Trilling's account a society that is republican, individualistic, and based on citizenship relies on a strong sentiment of self that each person must develop and protect.[18] Each must become himself, know himself, and express himself in his public choices. Each must, to use the political term, *represent* himself, thus the intense civic importance of complete self-knowledge and sincerity. The essence of acting is, of course, representing what one is not, simulating anger one does not feel, weeping tears at twenty past nine night after night, convincingly representing one night a miserly landlord and the next a benign and courageous doctor. To value and foster the skills of the actor is to reward those able to not-be themselves, not feel what they in fact feel·and, therefore, to strike at the heart of a social order based on full individual being and public self-representation.

As Rousseau pointed out, many consequences follow: the conversion of leisure from participatory to spectator experiences; the obsessive centralization of the feelings around the passion of love to the exclusion of more social feelings such as loyalty, friendship, and familial piety because of the dramatic suitability of sexual love; and, finally, the concentration of the theater on the actress.[19] This final consequence is due to the paradox of female virtue, in its ordinary domestic modesty and retirement, electrifying the theater with the energies of moral reversal.

The intuitive genius that Dreiser brings to his account of the theater and its central position as an image—like the rocking chair or the newspaper—for a description of American society is confirmed by the detailed interconnection of Rousseau's speculations and Dreiser's novel. To note only two characteristics here beyond those that are already obvious will suffice. Carrie's blankness, her lack of attachment or even mood, her easy forgetting of her family, her sister, Drouet, and even her disinterest in ever returning even for a visit, her passivity, and her ability to be almost hypnotized into acting under the gaze of Drouet, even her absence of desires as proved by her realization once she has a great deal of money that there is nothing that she wants to buy: all of these elements of blankness correspond to the assumption that Rousseau made that the more successful one were at acting the less one would have a sentiment of self. Secondly, the obsessive love interest of all of the parts played by Carrie, for which the best example is the harem girl that she plays in New York, goes along with a romantic deadness, a lack of erotic quality in her relations with men.[20] The audience's obvious fantasy of being in love with the actress that they pay to watch display her feelings is the relocated eroticism that has now disappeared from their actual lives. The most intense erotic moment of Dreiser's novel occurs when both Hurstwood, from his box in the audience, and Drouet backstage rise to a pitch of desire for Carrie beyond what they have ever felt in reality as they watch her play the part of Laura in the Elk's Club play. Similarly, as the frowning Quakeress in New York, Carrie faces an audience whose key can be found in the aging businessmen rich enough to buy the best tickets. "The portly gentlemen in the front rows began to feel that she was a delicious little morsel. It was the kind of frown that they would have loved to force away with kisses. All the gentlemen yearned towards her" (401). This erotic pleading, controlled and merchandized, is precisely what Dreiser had described earlier as Carrie's own relation to the clothes in department stores.

> When she came within earshot of their pleading [that of the clothes] desire in her bent a willing ear. The voice of the so-called inanimate! Who shall translate for us the language of the stones?
>
> "My dear," said the lace collar she secured from Partriges, "I fit you beautifully, don't give me up."
>
> "Ah such little feet," said the leather of the soft new shoes, "how effectively I cover them. What a pity they should ever want my aid." (94)

The erotic helplessness and need is what both actress and audience, objects and shopper, court one another with across the barriers of sales and theater tickets.

The sexualized quality of acting, protected as it is by fantasy and the barrier of the stage that separates the beloved actress from the numerous fantasizing suitors in the audience repeats the paradox mentioned earlier that sheltered within the fiction of her role the actress sells precisely the vitality of her personality. Intimacy of self-presence and intimacy of sexual relation are both paradoxically present in the neutralized, stage-lit world of pretence. One of the first consequences of Carrie's success as an actress is that she begins to receive a regular stream of marriage proposals from men who know nothing of her but what they have seen in her performance.

Where Dreiser goes beyond Rousseau is in his refusal to contrast acting with sincerity, his refusal to oppose the representation of what one is not to authentic self-representation. Dreiser is the first novelist to base his entire sense of the self on the dramatic possibilities inherent in a dynamic society. Acting involves primarily in Dreiser not deception but practice, not insincerity but installment payments on the world of possibility. In *Sister Carrie* acting is a constant social tactic. As a mockery of sincerity the words that provide Carrie's break into a speaking part in New York and therefore her rise to stardom are significant ones. To the Vizier past whom she is being paraded as one of the harem girls she says, in answer to his idle question, "Well, who are you?" "I am yours, truly" (387). In the very sassy pertness with which she improvises her answer she marks herself as a free and independent woman while her words (her part) declare her a slave. The final word "truly" caps the elegance of this paradoxical moment. To some extent acting in *Sister Carrie* always serves to preserve a freedom of the self from its appearance, and it is to that degree that it records a higher version of the possible or prospective self in defiance of the momentary "role" or "part" that it is compelled to play and be recognized in. When Carrie first sets out to find work in Chicago "she became conscious of being gazed upon and understood for what she was—a wage-seeker. . . . To avoid a certain indefinable shame she felt at being caught spying about for a position, she quickened her steps and assumed an air of indifference supposedly common to one on an errand" (18). She acts the role of one on an errand to avoid the collapse of recognition on the part of others that would freeze her into *no more than* what she happens to be in this momentary role of job seeker. Her acting is a protest on the part of the wider possibilities of her self. Similarly, Hurstwood in decline refuses to go home. "No, he would not go back there this evening. He would stay out and knock around *as a man who* was independent—not broke—well might. He bought a cigar, and went outside on the corner, where other individuals were lounging—brokers, racing people, thespians—his own flesh and blood" (330). It is the cigar that is the costume of this role. The ability to waste money on cigars proves that he is "independent" and not a destitute drifter.

Even when people appear just as they are they play their appearance as a role. Carrie "looked the well groomed woman of twenty-one" (286). This is exactly what she is. Nevertheless, a small distance occurs so that it is more accurate to say that she looked the part of a well-dressed woman of twenty-one rather than that she was. The diners at Sherries restaurant act the part of diners, "all were extremely noticeable." What goes on in the restaurant is an "exhibit of showy wasteful dining." The word "showy" is used many times in the novel to mark the conversion of experience into performance. In Chicago Mrs. Hurstwood wanted to "exhibit" her daughter Jessica since it had become time for the part of encouraging suitors. The force of the term "conspicuous" in the phrase "conspicuous consumption" invented by the Chicago sociologist and economist Veblen in the early years of Dreiser's career is here interpreted with great nuance. However, it is not at all consumption that is conspicuous, but anticipatory states of the self.

The importance of clothes in *Sister Carrie* arises from the choice that one can exercise over them as a conspicuous performance of prospective being. Drouet seduces Carrie by buying her the clothes that would be the appropriate costume only for the role of his mistress. The clothes are ones that she could not even explain let alone wear were she to stay in her role of working girl at her sister's flat. Similarly, Carrie's first acting jobs in New York translate into the paradoxical ability to buy the clothes for the role of a young actress. On the other side, Hurstwood's shabby clothes *expose* his state, the opposite but equally conspicuous equivalent to the *display* of state that is the normal function of clothes. Because clothes can be changed more rapidly than apartments they become a more sensitive index to changes of state. Clothes are one's address. Finally, only hotels are places of living sensitive enough to the fluctuations of self to equal clothing as performances of the momentary condition of the self. In New York after they separate, both Carrie and Hurstwood move through opposite ends of the spectrum of hotels. This hunger for day-by-day accounts of the fluctuation of fortune records the need of a society in which money will be kept in the stock market so that its waverings of value can be represented in the daily newspaper rather than in land or goods which are, by comparison, subject only to year-long or decade-long readings of change of worth. As the rocking chair is to fortune's wheel, second by second rises and falls, so too are clothes, hotels, and newspapers to the long-term indexes of fortune and value.

6. The Plot of Decline

In writing *Sister Carrie* Dreiser made two profound structural decisions that are in fact related to the tragic ambitions of his work. *Sister Carrie*, like Dreiser's one other great novel, might have been titled *An American Tragedy* and in both novels there is special emphasis on the renewed meaning given to tragedy by the dynamics of American life. The essential structural decisions are: first, the division of the novel into two halves, the first taking place in Chicago, the second in New York. The second decision divided the New York half into a balanced and closely modeled double story that compels us to see and comprehend the rise of Carrie by means of the fall of Hurstwood.

In the Chicago portion of the novel we have a familiar 19th-century *Bildungsroman* of the orphan. Arriving in the city, relying only on the intangible energy of her nature, Carrie is the one dynamic, unsettled figure in a world where everyone else represents terminal points, places and levels at which she might arrive and stabilize herself. The Hansons, Drouet, and Hurstwood are the three alternative fixed destinations each soliciting, in effect, the orphan with the implicit question: "Isn't this enough? Can't you be satisfied to stop here?" They themselves are static (in Chicago) and only Carrie is in motion. Society is conceived of as a set of levels with different types and value systems. Chicago is a social comedy of mobility sketched between honest, hard-working immigrant toilers whose lives are decent and respectable, grim and pleasureless; and managers at the upper levels of a nightclub large enough to have five bartenders and the big men at the Elks Club. That is the complete social range. Drouet is the dead center of the scale.

New York is not an extension of this social scale into both higher and lower possibilities. It is an entirely new world, one that is a symbolic simplification into either-or choices. All processes are speeded up and an inevitable pair of slopes appear: youth and age, not-yet and has-been, celebrity and nobody, female and male, stage lights and total darkness, Broadway and Bowery. The second half of the novel is an absolute world, not a portrayal of a society of layers and alternative values. All that remain are inside and outside, rising and falling, fame and death. In New York not only is Carrie dynamic but she is seen against a social system which has only dynamic possibilities. There is no place as such in this world.

Like all tragic settings Dreiser's New York is a figuration of time and not space. It is composed of stages rather than locations. Here the *Bildungsroman* plot has lost all force, for it is a progressive, optimistic plot that is exploratory, comic, and essentially a plot of growth in which the central figure finds a concrete world that by means of marriage, work, home, and social position substantiates the youthful inner possibilities by solidifying them into the facts of a life history. Instead New York is governed by the decisive contribution of Naturalism to the small stock of curves for human action: the plot of decline. The plot of decline characterizes many of the central novels of the last decades of the 19th century. Hardy's *Jude the Obscure*, Zola's *L'Assomoir* and Dreiser's *Sister Carrie* are its masterpieces and Mann's *Buddenbrooks* is its intergenerational epic. These plots of exhaustion have as their central subject the realm of energy rather than value. They revolve around strength and weakness, not good and evil. Their essential matters are youth and age, freshness and exhaustion. Behind the plot of decline is the Darwinian description of struggle, survival, and extinction. Darwinism has the characteristic as a theory that it is more and more optimistic about larger and larger categories, more and more pessimistic as you reach down to more local or individual events. Species sometimes survive, individuals never, and even species often perish while the total balance of species, adapted to the facts of the environment, improves even at the cost of species, just as species improve even at the cost of individuals. The most acute pessimism arises from a consideration of the individual life cycle as one that rises from the helplessness of infancy to the capacity to ensure individual survival and then declining from that point to death. The primary question for the Naturalist plot is whether the division of life into these two stages (rise and decline) is one of a very long rise that reaches, as it often does in social or financial terms, to the age of sixty, and then follows a short decline. Or is the proportion reversed as it is in the body's strength, a rapid rise peaking at twenty and a long continuous decline that takes up the longest section of personal history? In Darwinian terms, this latter possibility would be a brief rise to the moment of reproduction in the twenties and then a long superfluous decline. The Naturalist plot of decline in Hardy, Zola, and Dreiser bases itself to a large extent on the history of the body and not that of social position. It is therefore a chronicle of subtraction and weakening based on energy, sexuality, and the conversion of freshness to exhaustion.

One of Dreiser's curious emphases is on Hurstwood's age. He is never able to sweep Carrie away emotionally.

> This was due to a lack of power on his part, a lack of that majesty of passion that sweeps the mind from its seat, fuses and melts all arguments and theories into a tangled mass, and destroys for the time being the reasoning power. This majesty of passion is possessed by nearly every man once in his life, but it is usually an attribute of youth and conduces to the first successful mating.
>
> Hurstwood, being an older man, could scarcely be said to retain the fire of youth, though he did possess a passion warm and unreasoning. (199)

This older man is in fact 39, but Dreiser's point is a Darwinian one that refers to mating rather than to feelings or passions as they occur in the mind. The goal of the single youthful urgency is reproduction, not sexual enjoyment as an experience, and Hurstwood's early marriage led to children as his later affair with Carrie does not.

Only a few years later in New York, "he looked haggard around the eyes and quite old." At the age of 43 he is comfortably built and so "walking was not easy" (310). Carrie begins to draw away from him because "she began to see that he was gloomy and taciturn, not a young strong and buoyant man. He looked a little bit old to her about the eyes and mouth now" (300). His habits are those of a retired and sedentary man of sixty. He reads the newspapers all day, becomes a chair-warmer in the comfortable hotel lobbies and parcels out his money like a frugal pensioner who gives up the daily shave so as to have a cigar now and then. What might seem an exaggeration here is in fact a speeding up, a compression of effects much like the rapid rise of Carrie to fame. One component of a tragic rendering of events lies in compressing the inevitable and the incremental into a few shattering or magical events. Thus Hurstwood's theft, which might be viewed as the cause of his destiny in New York, and so it would be if the order of Dreiser's world were a moral rather than a Darwinian and economic order, is in fact only a notation in compressed form of the inevitability, at some point, in his life of a balanced moment at which he teeters unaware that he is no longer rising but beginning to fall. The theft is a registration of the almost physical nausea, as on a swing or a ferris wheel, at that point where effort has ceased and in an instant gravity takes over to pull one towards the earth. Dreiser's theory of rise and fall is offered in the best long analytic passage of his novel, the opening three pages of Chapter 33, a chapter with the half title "The Slope of the Years."

> A man's fortune or material progress is very much the same as his bodily growth. Either he is growing stronger, healthier, wiser as the youth approaching manhood, or he is growing weaker, older, less incisive mentally as the man approaching old age. There are no other states. Frequently there is a period between the cessation of youthful accretion and the setting in, in the case of the middle-aged man, of the tendency toward decay when the two processes are almost perfectly balanced and there is little doing in either direction. Given time enough, however, the balance becomes a sagging to the grave side. (295–6)

Dreiser continues by pointing out that every great fortune, made in youth and in fact representing the conversion of personal energy into money, would inevitably be depleted and lost by the weakened power of decision as the owner of the fortune aged, except that such men always conscript younger minds and energies and buy up their vitality. These words interpret precisely what happens as Hurstwood flees Chicago with the stolen energy that is represented both by the stolen money and by the stock of Carrie's vitality that he has also stolen from Drouet. Early in the novel Dreiser refers to money as "honestly stored energy" and it is to that extent the body's way of spreading out its stock of youthful energy throughout a life too long for its actual store. Hurstwood's theft is the exact double of his relationship with Carrie: in each he appropriates the energies of others. Neither the theft nor the affair is the cause of his fall, because the fall of which Dreiser is speaking is the inevitable fall of vitality over time. Instead both the affair and the theft are desperate attempts to stave off, once falling has begun, temporarily and by means of stolen energies, the rapid sinking that converts the hopeful into the hopeless.

Hurstwood's relation to Carrie is only the intimate form of the wider social fact represented by her relation to her audience: a social group of aging males whose stored energy in the form of money now disguises the actual exhaustion of their spirits. What they rent in the theater is her vitality and youth and not at all her talent or remarkable beauty. Dreiser is careful to give Carrie no particular talent, only the traits that are those of youth itself: freshness, hopefulness, confidence, the imitative skills that are those of children and the unclouded flexibility of those who have as yet no concrete world that they would not give up for the chance at something better. She is the "not-yet" to which the only other term is "has-been." In the theater these two feed off one another as actress and audience who exchange energy for the honestly stored energy of money.

In Dreiser's novel even Carrie's sister Minnie at twenty-seven looks old and used up. The division is that of the body which reaches its full height at nineteen or twenty and shrinks from then on to death. This life history is that of products and objects which are best when new or fresh and then become worn out and discarded. The life history of a shirt is one of continual decline. All goods are used up and replaced. Within *Sister Carrie* relationships, houses, cities, and especially living situations are discarded in the way clothing might be. Hurstwood himself is worn out rather than captured and submitted to moral or legal defeat. He is obsolete like a pair of shoes rather than aged like a man. He is a left-over and a scrap. The Bowery of New York is a collective heap of discarded men. By the end of the novel he is not so much dead as extinct.

Hurstwood's decline is measured by the shrinking of his space from a Chicago mansion to a modest apartment to a smaller flat to a room to a cubicle, and it is measured equally by the melting away of his savings, or rather his stolen savings: $1300 when he reaches New York, $500 by Chapter 33, $340 in Chapter 36, $100 and then $50 in Chapter 37, then finally he is a beggar for dimes and beds for a night. An equation is made between the decline of his health, his eyesight, the amount of light in his world and the shrinking of his money.

Throughout his decline the single act that Dreiser repeats again and again is his reading of the newspaper. Reading becomes the partner term to the acting associated with rising, hopeful, prospective being. The newspaper possesses its reader with lives and events not his own in much the same way that a role does an actress. The newspaper is in fact a mediating object in New York. Hurstwood's only desire seems to be to go on reading it, Carrie's highest desire is to be featured in it. Breaking into the theater seems only a halfway point to breaking into the newspapers. The newspaper is retrospective, defining what happened yesterday. It is literally about what "has been." As Hurstwood reaches his nadir he is forced to root around for out-of-date newspapers to try to see if there is any news about Carrie.

Dreiser speaks of Hurstwood as "buried in his papers." On a park bench the newspaper is the blanket of the down-and-out tramp. When he no longer consorts with celebrities he reads about them in the newspaper stories. Once Carrie has gone she begins to appear in the papers and he can follow her there. The newspaper becomes a way of not quite dying to a life that he no longer lives. In one of those very lovely in-conspicuous scenes that mark Dreiser's work at its best, Hurst-wood, so cut off from the world that he would rather not look out the window, reads in the newspapers that a bad storm is due, then in later editions that it has begun, then that it is a record storm, then that it will end soon, and finally, that it has ended. To follow stars and celebrities whø are in fact in-accessible is here put in its proper frame of meaning: the newspaper is the essential symbol of decline because it involves a preference for all experience as retrospective rather than lived, even the experience of a storm. The disappearance of Carrie from Hurstwood's life is brilliantly done, not by an article in the newspaper, but by the physical object of the paper itself. "He knew that Carrie was not there not only because there was no light shown through the transom, but because the evening papers were stuck between the outside knob and the door" (394).

The resonant final third of Dreiser's novel does not link the stories of Hurstwood and Carrie by way of contrast, that is only the superficial social level of what is in fact a tragic inevitability, because Carrie's rise, representing as it does youth itself, and Hurstwood's decline, no more than a com-pressed account of age itself, are stages that magnify by means of "star" and "tramp" the inevitable small-scale rise and fall that together make up the life history of the self considered as energy. By means of two characters Dreiser can make simul-taneous what is in actual experience consecutive, locating in two persons the prospective and retrospective phases of one life. To achieve this he carefully matches their lives as super-ficial contrasts connecting deep structural similarities.

Near the end Hurstwood lives at the Broadway Central Hotel. At this point they each live, as a favor, in a hotel where neither really pays. He lives there as a favor to him (a charity) on the part of the kindly manager. She lives there as a favor to the hotel (an advertisement). Carrie's meals are bought for her by men who compete for the privilege. Hurstwood's too are free at soup kitchens or as a result of begging from these same prosperous gentlemen. The public buys tickets to see Carrie and outside the theater they also buy tickets at the solicitation of the ex-soldier who harangues them to contribute the price of bed tickets for the hundreds of homeless men that he lines up like a chorus line, Hurstwood among them. Hurstwood marches down Broadway in an army of tramps and Carrie marches back and forth on stage in a harem of chorus girls. Carrie has won for herself a place in the chorus line and Hurstwood's life is made of calculations of his place in the soup lines, bread lines, and shelter lines.

Hurstwood's one final job as a strike-breaker is in fact described as a performance. We see him rehearse his role, practicing with the trolley in the yards just as Carrie practices her moves as a chorus girl. The strike-breaking "play" is performed by running the streetcar with two policemen on board through a hostile audience of strikers and their families who jeer and hoot as though at a bad opera. The streetcar runs are fictional and symbolic since their purpose is not to carry passengers but to break the strike by demonstrating to the public, via the newspapers that all of the strikers have lost their "parts" and have been replaced in their roles by new actors, men simulating drivers. Hurstwood spends a day rehearsing, then goes out to play his role on the city streets. He is pelted like a bad actor and runs offstage in mid-performance, abandoning his role as motorman or, as the strikers name his role, "scab." When he gets cold on the trolley "he shivered, stamped his feet, and beat his arms as he had seen other motormen do in the past" (382). His play is woven by Dreiser directly into Carrie's rehearsals, performances, and breakthroughs. He is pelted off the stage just on the day when she speaks for the first time and begins her rise to stardom. The strike is the aging performer's nightmare, just as Carrie's rise is the neophyte's dream. Dreiser's highly conscious repetition of elements in the two lives derives from his intention that they be seen as stages. Throughout his novel "Carrie" has only a first name and "Hurstwood" has only a last. They are first and last names that combine to make one life; first stage and last stage, rise and fall of fortune's wheel.

Notes

INTRODUCTION

1. Leo Marx, *The Machine in the Garden* (New York: Oxford University Press, 1964), 142.
2. György Lukács, *The Historical Novel*, trans. Hannah and Stanley Mitchell (Boston: Beacon Press, 1962).
3. In addition to Lukács see Steven Marcus, *Representations* (New York: Random House, 1975) especially the two essays "Awaking from the Nightmare? Notes on the Historical Novel" and "Literature and Social Theory: Starting in with George Eliot."
4. Victor Shklovsky, "Art as Technique" in *Russian Formalist Criticism; Four Essays*, trans. Lee T. Lemon and Marion J. Reis (Lincoln: University of Nebraska Press, 1965).

CHAPTER 1

1. The phrase was first used by John L. O'Sullivan in the July 1845 issue of his *United States Magazine and Democratic Review*.
2. Alexis de Tocqueville, *Democracy in America,* The Henry Reeve text as revised by Francis Bowen (New York: A. A. Knopf, 1980), 452.
3. Francis Parkman, *The Conspiracy of Pontiac*, The Centenary Edition (Boston: Little Brown, and Company, 1926), 2:331.
4. Ibid., 1:IX.
5. Henry Wadsworth Longfellow, *The Poetical Works of Henry*

Wadsworth Longfellow, 6 vols. (New York: AMS Press, 1966), 2:281.

6. Jean-Jacques Rousseau, *Emile*, trans. with Introduction and Notes by Allan Bloom (New York: Basic Books, 1979), 98–99.

7. Robert Frost, *The Poetry of Robert Frost*, ed. Edward Connery Lathem (New York: Holt, Rinehart and Winston, 1969), 245.

8. Tocqueville, *Democracy in America*, 26.

9. Parkman, *The Conspiracy of Pontiac*, 2:140–63.

10. Ibid., 140–41.

11. Ibid., 324.

12. The chapter on Cooper in D. H. Lawrence's *Studies in Classic American Literature* (London: Thomas Seltzer, 1923) is the essential treatment of the subject of killing. Cooper's novel has, following Lawrence, been given an important analysis by Yvor Winters in his *In Defense of Reason* (Denver: A Swallow Press Book, University of Denver Press, 1947). See also Roy Harvey Pearce, *Savagism and Civilization* (Baltimore: The Johns Hopkins University Press, 1953) and R. W. B. Lewis, *The American Adam* (Chicago: University of Chicago Press, 1955).

13. For the Jacksonian policy and its consequences see William Christie MacLeod, *The American Indian Frontier* (New York: A. A. Knopf, 1928), Robert Berkhofer, *The White Man's Indian* (New York: A. A. Knopf, 1978), Michael Paul Rogin, *Fathers and Children* (New York: A. A. Knopf, 1975), Grant Forman, *The Five Civilized Tribes* (Norman: University of Oklahoma Press, 1934).

14. Francis Parkman, *The Oregon Trail*, ed. E. N. Feltskog (Madison: University of Wisconsin Press, 1969), 96.

15. James Fenimore Cooper, *The Deerslayer*, the Darley Edition (New York: D. Appleton and Company, 1914), 15–16. All future references to *The Deerslayer* will be indicated by page number at the end of the quote.

16. The point is made in Sir Isaiah Berlin, *Four Essays on Liberty* (London: Oxford University Press, 1969).

17. McLeod, *The American Indian Frontier*, 505–32.

18. Tocqueville, *Democracy in America*, 26.

19. For alternative readings of this crucial scene, see Winters, *In Defense of Reason*, and Pearce, *Savagism and Civilization*.

20. Tocqueville makes this point in showing the success of the English and the great failure of the French. See his Chapter 18, "The Present and Probable Future Condition of the Three Races That Inhabit the Territory of the United States" in *Democracy in America*, vol. 1.

21. The analysis of elipsis as a key element of narrative time was developed by Gérard Genette in *Figures III* (Paris: Editions du Seuil, 1972), 122–45.

22. John David Unruh, *The Plains Across: The Overland Emigrants and the Trans-Mississippi West, 1840–60* (Urbana: University of Illinois Press, 1979), 124.

23. Blake Nevius, *Cooper's Landscapes: An Essay on the Picturesque Vision* (Berkeley and Los Angeles: University of California Press, 1976).

24. Parkman, *The Conspiracy of Pontiac*, 1:x.

25. The line is from his poem "A Prayer for My Daughter," W. B. Yeats, *Collected Poems* (London: MacMillan and Company, 1950), 213.

CHAPTER 2

1. See Henry Nash Smith, *Virgin Land* (Cambridge: Harvard University Press, 1950) especially bk. 3. See also Leo Marx, *The Machine in the Garden* (New York: Oxford University Press, 1964).

2. Quoted in Smith, 142.

3. Harriet Beecher Stowe, *Uncle Tom's Cabin* (Boston: Houghton Mifflin, The Riverside Library), 149. All future references to the novel will be indicated by page numbers immediately following the quotation.

4. Quoted in Smith, 142.

5. Leo Tolstoy, *What is Art*, trans. Almyer Maude (New York: Liberal Arts Press, 1960).

6. See R. S. Crane, "Suggestions Toward a Geneology of the 'Man of Feeling'" *ELH*, I (1934):205–30 and Louis Bredvold, *The*

Natural History of Sensibility (Detroit: Wayne State University Press, 1962) and Northrop Frye, "Toward Defining an Age of Sensibility," in James Clifford, ed., *Eighteenth-Century English Literature, Modern Essays in Criticism* (New York: Oxford University Press, 1959).

7. Except in the case of women. See Ann Douglas, *The Feminization of American Culture* (New York: A. A. Knopf, 1977).

8. J. M. S. Tompkins, *The Popular Novel in England, 1770–1800* (London: Constable & Co., Ltd., 1932).

9. See among others Lawrence Stone, *The Family, Sex and Marriage: England 1500–1800* (New York: Harper & Row, 1977) and Edward Shorter, *The Making of the Modern Family* (New York: Basic Books, 1975).

10. Rousseau, "Discourse on the Origin and Foundations of Inequality Among Men," in *The First and Second Discourses*, ed. by Roger Masters, trans. Roger D. Masters and Judith R. Masters (New York: St. Martin Press, 1964), 104–20.

11. *Ibid.*, 131. Rousseau borrows the image from Mandeville's *The Fable of the Bees*. His analysis is striking because the image is one of the only ones in the "Discourse on Inequality."

12. Wordsworth created the notion of the personality as a ruin. The importance of time in this notion can be seen by considering how we always imagine that we can mitigate or compensate for a catastrophe that has recently happened, but when we meet someone to whom a disaster occurred many years ago we do not imagine we can provide relief if no one in so many years has been able to do so and if time itself has not lessened the effects. Only at this point can we say that an ultimate crime has been committed or an ultimate disaster experienced. Only then are we as listeners in the sentimental relation to the other's suffering.

13. Prue's story, which occurs at the end of Chapter 18, is retold to Little Eva and is the immediate cause of her sickness and death.

14. The paradox that follows from this modest theory is that Stowe's novel is perhaps the single most effective political work of art in the history of literature.

15. Stowe, *Uncle Tom's Cabin*, 456.

16. Ibid., 177.

17. Ibid., 174–80.

CHAPTER 3

1. Theodore Dreiser, *Sister Carrie*, Rinehart Edition (New York: Holt, Rinehart & Winston, 1957), 15–16. All future quotations from the novel will be indicated parenthetically after the quote.

2. Charles Baudelaire, "L'Invitation au Voyage" in *Les Fleurs du Mal*, trans. Richard Howard (Boston: David R. Godine, 1982), 236.

3. Theodore Dreiser, *An American Tragedy* (New York: Boni and Liveright, 1925), 1:401. All future quotations from the novel will be indicated parenthetically after the quote.

4. Walter Benjamin, "On Some Motifs in Baudelaire," in *Illuminations*, ed. Hannah Arendt, trans. Harry Zohn (New York: Schocken, 1969).

5. Quoted in Walter Benjamin, *Reflections*, ed. Peter Demetz, trans. Edmund Jephcott (New York: Harcourt, Brace, Javanowich, 1978), 131.

6. Leonardo Benevolo, *History of Modern Architecture*, vol. 1 (Cambridge: The MIT Press, 1971), 145–47.

7. Georg Simmel, "The Metropolis and Mental Life," in *The Sociology of Georg Simmel*, ed. Kurt Wolff (Glencoe, Illinois: Free Press, 1950), 410–13.

8. Ulf Hannerz, *Exploring the City* (New York: Columbia University Press, 1980).

9. The classic studies are in effect a closely interwoven set of variations on the ideas of Simmel and Weber.

10. Louis Wirth, *On Cities and Social Life, Selected Papers*, ed. Albert J. Reiss, Jr. (Chicago: University of Chicago Press, 1964), 71.

11. Benevolo, *History of Modern Architecture*, 102.

12. Rudolf Arnheim, *The Dynamics of Architectural Form* (Berkeley: University of California Press, 1977), 227.

13. Henry Adams, *The Education of Henry Adams* (Boston: Houghton Mifflin, 1918), 340.

14. Giorgio Ciucci et al., *The American City, from the Civil War to the New Deal* (Cambridge: MIT Press, 1979), 29.

15. Sigfried Giedion, *Mechanization Takes Command* (New York: W. W. Norton, 1948), 396–405.

16. For an analysis of the relations between the spatial structure of newspapers and urban experience, see Philip Fisher, "City Matters: City Minds," in *The Worlds of Victorian Fiction*, ed. Jerome H. Buckley (Cambridge: Harvard University Press, 1975).

17. Lionel Trilling, *Sincerity and Authenticity* (Cambridge: Harvard University Press, 1973), 62–67.

18. Rousseau's description clearly distinguishes the actor from the orator or preacher. "When the orator appears in public, it is to speak or not to show himself off; he represents only himself; he fills only his own role, speaks only in his own name, says, or ought to say, only what he thinks; the man and the role being the same, he is in his place; he is in the situation of any citizen who fulfills the functions of his estate. But an actor on the stage, displaying other sentiments than his own, saying only what he is made to say, often representing a chimerical being, annihilates himself, as it were, and is lost in his hero. And in this forgetting of the man, if something remains of him it is used as the plaything of the spectators. What shall I say of those who seem to be afraid of having too much merit as they are and who degrade themselves to the point of playing characters whom they would be quite distressed to resemble." Jean-Jacques Rousseau, *Politics and the Arts: Letter to M. D'Alembert on the Theatre*, ed. and trans. Allan Bloom (Ithaca: Cornell University Press, 1960), 80–81.

19. Ibid., 82–92.

20. The role of harem girl exactly represents, in this case, the truth of the actress's relation to the audience. As we see from the many invitations that Carrie receives, the rich men in the audience who date chorus girls consider them a kind of harem that is literally on display for the audience's choice while being fictionally on display for the vizier's choice.

Index